CARPENTRY TOOLMAKING

CARPENTRY TOOLMAKING

An instructors' guide

AARON MOORE

INTERMEDIATE TECHNOLOGY PUBLICATIONS 1993

Intermediate Technology Publications Ltd,
103–105 Southampton Row, London WC1B 4HH, UK

© Intermediate Technology Publications 1993

A CIP record for this book is available from the British Library

ISBN 1 85339 196 4

Typeset by Inforum, Rowlands Castle, Hants
Printed in Great Britain by SRP Exeter

Contents

INTRODUCTION

This guide is intended for experienced carpenters who want to teach their tool-making skills to other people.

The system described here can be used when working with an apprentice in your own workshop, when running training courses in rural areas or when working as an instructor at a training centre. It is designed to help you to teach effectively on the basis of carefully prepared practical demonstrations.

It is important that toolmaking is taught methodically and systematically if the tools are to be of a sufficiently high standard. Each new technique must be demonstrated clearly and accurately before the trainees go on to practise the skill. Each demonstration should take less than ten minutes to complete, and end with questions and answers to make sure the demonstration has been understood. You should allow students to discover for themselves how and why tools work, and encourage them to develop modifications or even to design new tools.

Most of the session plans involve practical demonstrations, but there are a few workshop lessons which deal with important theoretical aspects of toolmaking. These should be dealt with as class discussions.

The first page of each set of demonstration plans consists of one perspective drawing and two dimensioned drawings; the second page gives a brief description of the tool and a drawing showing the names of the components. Each of the following pages gives all the information needed to demonstrate one process towards the construction of the tool. The drawing at the bottom of each page can easily be reproduced on a blackboard or chart, and shows the component after the demonstration has been completed.

Each set of plans contains all the demonstrations needed to make one tool, but you may decide that the students are capable of carrying out certain stages without being shown.

The tools described in the demonstration plans were developed to be made in situations where money is not available to equip a workshop with expensive, mass-produced tools. However, the preference for Western tools is now so deep-rooted that the introduction of handmade tools can be difficult and slow. The trainees should therefore use handmade tools from the very beginning of their training, so that they are accustomed to using them.

Introducing the project

Begin each new project with the information given on the second page of the plans. Tell the students:

○ WHAT they are going to make;
○ THE TIME needed to complete the tool;
○ WHY the tool is important and what it can be used for;
○ HOW the tool will be made.

Here it should be stated that each step in the construction of the tool will be demonstrated two or three times, and all students will complete each stage before the next stage will be started.

Next, demonstrate the tool. It should be shown to the group and its use demonstrated. One or two students can be given the chance to use it, if they have not done so already.

Finally, name each part. In most cases the tool consists of a number of pieces which should be named individually, with a description of each one's function.

The demonstrations

Each demonstration is conducted in the same way. Before the demonstration you should:

○ Prepare all the materials needed.
○ Collect all the tools and teaching aids required, and clear a workbench.
○ Check that students have prepared materials to practise the process, or have completed the previous stage satisfactorily.
○ Practise the demonstration quietly if it is the first attempt.

The students can then be asked to gather around the bench so that they can all hear and see you. Begin the demonstration by stating what is going to be demonstrated and why the demonstration is important. Tell the students what you are going to do, and to expect some questions at the end.

Whenever a new or complicated skill is being taught, it is a good idea to demonstrate the process three times:

○ Go through the process silently and at the same speed that you would carry out the operation if you were working on your own.

○ Demonstrate the actions slowly and deliberately, describing the process and emphasizing the relevant points.

○ Repeat the operation at normal speed, but this time asking questions about the process. These questions should be aimed at emphasizing the information you wish to put across.

This method allows the students to see how the processes are carried out under normal conditions; they can take in the information aurally, and they can test their understanding by answering questions. The questions also test the effectiveness of the demonstration.

If there is time to make three full demonstrations, three sets of materials should be prepared in advance. In cases where it would take more than ten minutes to go through the process three times – for example, cutting a mortise – the demonstration should be split into three stages. The first series of cuts can be made silently; the next, slowly, with a description of the process; and the final series of cuts can be accompanied by questions. It is up to you to decide how best to conduct each session.

Order of teaching

It is recommended that the simpler tools are taught first, and that the order of instruction should therefore be as the tools appear in the book:

○ Try-square
○ Mortise gauge
○ Bow-saw
○ Sash clamp

○ Bench clamp
○ Rebate plane
○ Smoothing plane
○ Jack plane
○ Plough plane
○ Workbench and vice.

There is an appendix of teaching plans for forge work, for the production of cutting tools. Blacksmithing techniques can obviously be attempted only if the necessary tools and equipment are available.

Using the tools

In order to overcome the prejudice against handmade tools it is important that you encourage the trainees to use the tools they have made. Whenever possible the tools should be taught in conjunction with other course work; for example, before making a window casement or a picture frame the students can make a rebate plane with which to cut the rebates necessary for both such projects.

TRY-SQUARE

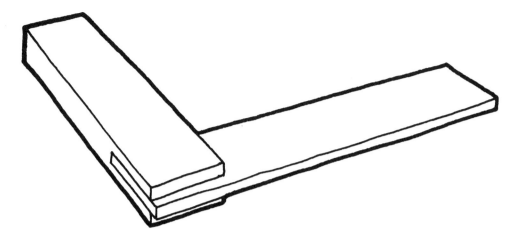

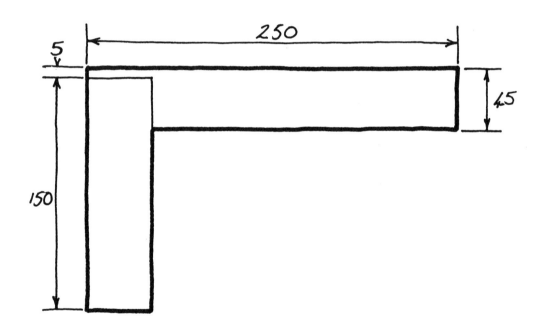

4   *Try-square*

Objective

At the end of this session each participant will have made a try-square.

Previous knowledge assumed

Competence in: preparing timber, marking out and cutting bridle joints.

Tools required

Try-square
Pencil
Jack plane
Marking gauge
Tenon-saw
6mm chisel
Mallet
Steel rule or tape measure

Common problems

Cutting the bridle joint
Using a blunt chisel to remove the waste in the bridle joint
Setting of blade and stock when gluing up

Cutting list

The instructor and students need to prepare hardwood timber to the following dimensions (mm):

ITEM	QUANTITY	MATERIAL	L	W	T
Stock	1	Hardwood	150	45	20
Blade	1	Hardwood	250	45	6

Also needed

PVA wood glue

Introduction

Time   One day.

What   In this session we are all going to make a try-square.

Why   It is an important tool which is used for marking out joints
              and testing timber for squareness. Without a try-square you
              cannot make joinery or furniture that is strong and looks
              good.
                 A wooden square will not last as long as one with a steel
              blade and it must be used with care, but it is quick and easy
              to make.

How   The session will consist of a series of demonstrations. Each
              step will be demonstrated two or three times. I will ask some
              questions to check that the demonstration was clear, then
              you will practise the same operation. We will wait until
              everyone is finished before the next step is demonstrated.

This is the try-square we are going to make. [SHOW TOOL TO TRAINEES]
You use it in the same way as a manufactured try-square.

These are the parts.

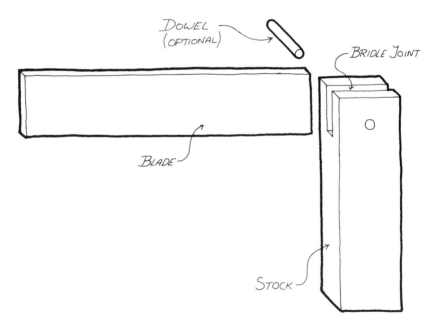

DEMO 1 Marking out the stock

Why   So that the bridle joint can be cut.

Materials   One piece of hardwood 150 × 45 × 20mm (stock); one piece of hardwood 250 × 45 × 6mm (blade).

Tools   Try-square; tape measure/ruler; marking gauge; pencil.

ACTIONS

1. Use a try-square and pencil to mark a line all round the stock, 40mm from one end. This marks the depth of the socket into which the blade will fit.

2. Use a marking gauge to mark the cheeks of the socket. It should be 6mm wide and centred in the edge of the stock. Set the marking gauge first to 7mm, and then to 13mm, to produce the right size of socket.

3. Check that the marking out is correct by holding the blade up to the stock.

4. Mark the waste.

POINTS FOR EMPHASIS

○ All marking out must be done from the face side or the face edge.

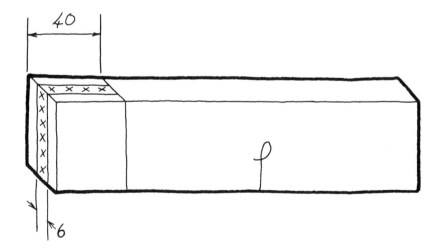

DEMO 2 Cutting the bridle joint

Why   So that the blade can be jointed to the stock.

Materials   Workpieces from the last demonstration.

Tools   Tenon-saw; 6mm chisel; mallet or hammer.

ACTIONS

1. Place the stock in the vice at an angle sloping away from you. Position the tenon-saw to the waste side of the gauge line and saw horizontally down to the pencil line. Saw down both sides of the socket.

2. Turn the stock round and replace it vertically in the vice to finish the cut.

3. Use a chisel with a mallet or a hammer to remove the waste from the socket. Place the chisel close to the line with the bevel facing towards the end and strike the handle. Move the chisel a few millimetres towards the end and strike again to cut a small wedge of waste. Repeat until you have cut halfway through and turn the stock over to work from the other side.

4. Clean up the end of the socket and check that it is flat using a straight edge.

POINTS FOR EMPHASIS

○ Saw down the waste side of the line.
○ Do not saw below the pencil line.
○ This method of sawing the joint allows you to see both edges as they are being sawn. The kerf of the first cut will guide the saw at the far side.
○ A sharp chisel is needed to remove the waste.

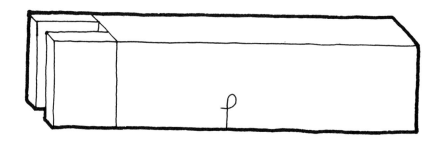

8 *Try-square*

DEMO 3   Assembling the square

Why   To fix the two parts of the stock firmly in position.

Materials   Workpieces from the last demonstration; wood glue; wet cloth; two clamping blocks.

Tools   Try-square; 'G' clamp; jack plane; wheel brace; 6mm twist bit.

ACTIONS

1. Fit the blade into the stock without glue, checking that the joining surfaces are touching. Make sure that the stock and the blade form a right angle: use a try-square that you know is true. If there is a problem you can still chisel out the end of the socket.

2. Apply a thin layer of glue to all areas of the joint and assemble the parts.

3. Test that the blade and the stock are square, then clamp the joint with a 'G' clamp. Check once again that the two parts are square and wipe off any excess glue with a wet rag.

4. Once the glue is dry, a 6mm hole can be drilled through the centre of the joint and a small dowel glued in place to give the joint extra strength.

5. Plane the end grain of the blade flush with the back of the stock and clean up the ends of the dowel.

POINTS FOR EMPHASIS

o   The two parts of the joint must be square.
o   Wood glue works only when the two parts of the joint are in contact.

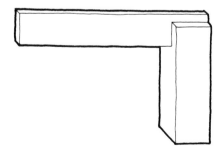

Try-square   9

DEMO 4   Testing the try-square

Why   It is important to know that the try-square being used is
                 accurate.

Materials   One piece of scrap timber roughly 300 × 150 × 20mm, planed
                 face side and face edge.

Tools   The finished try-square; pencil.

ACTIONS

1. Take a piece of wood about 200mm wide, with the face side and the face
    edge planed straight and square.

2. Place the try-square on the timber and draw a line from the face edge.

3. Turn the try-square over and approach the line from the other side.

POINTS FOR EMPHASIS

o   If the square is true, the pencil line and the straight edge will be parallel to
    each other.
o   Make sure the stock of the square is held against the face edge every time it
    is used.

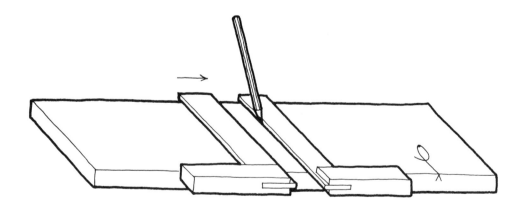

MORTISE GAUGE

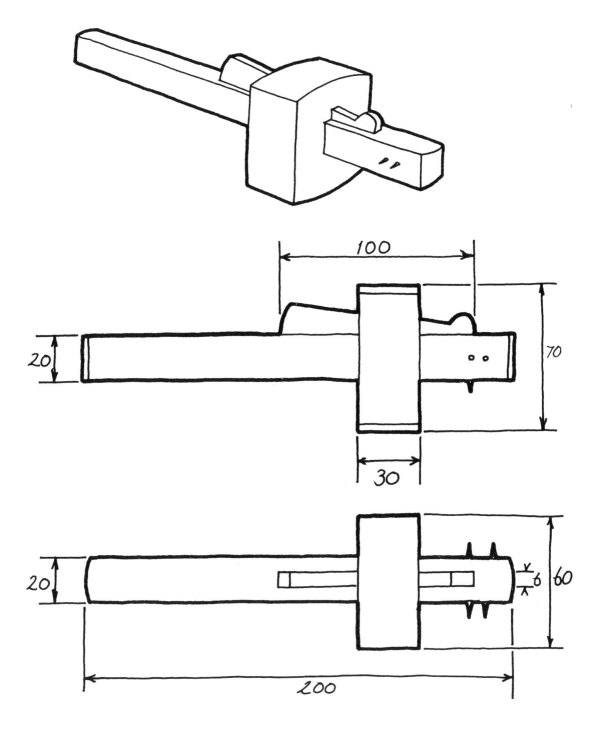

100

20

70

30

20

6

60

200

Objective

At the end of this session each participant will have made a mortise gauge.

Previous knowledge assumed

Competence in: preparing timber, marking out and cutting mortise and tenon joints.

Tools required

Try-square
Pencil
Steel rule or tape measure
Jack plane
Marking gauge
6mm chisel

12mm chisel
Mallet
Pin hammer
Tenon-saw
Pincers
Saw file

Common problems

Using a blunt chisel to cut the mortise in the stock
Cutting the mortise too big
Fitting the stem
Shaping the stock

Cutting list

The instructor and each student need to prepare hardwood timber to the following dimensions (mm):

ITEM	QUANTITY	MATERIAL	L	W	T
Stem	1	Hardwood	200	22	22
Stock	1	Hardwood	200	60	30
Wedge	1	Hardwood	100	15	6

Also needed

Five 25mm wire nails

Introduction

Time　　　　One day.

What　　　　In this session we are all going to make a simple mortise gauge.

Why　　　　Gauges are essential tools if joints are to be marked out and cut accurately. They are used for marking lines parallel to the face side or face edge of a piece of timber, and have two main uses:

　　　　　　o　To mark timber before planing it to width and thickness;
　　　　　　o　For marking out the pins and sockets of joints.

How　　　　The session will be made up of a series of demonstrations. Each step will be demonstrated two or three times. I will ask some questions to check that the demonstration was clear, then you will practise the same operation. We will wait until everyone is finished before the next step is demonstrated.

This is the mortise gauge we are going to make. [SHOW TOOL TO TRAINEES] It works like this.

These are the parts.

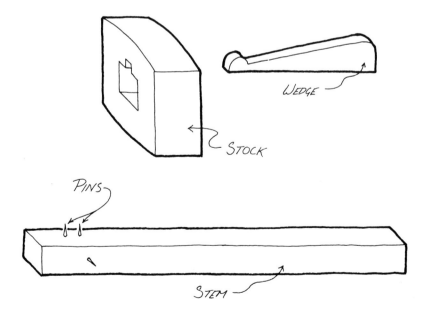

DEMO 1   Marking out the stock

Why   So that the mortise can be cut to let the stem into the stock.

Materials   One piece of hardwood 200 × 60 × 30mm.

Tools   Try-square; marking gauge; pencil; tape measure.

ACTIONS

1. Square lines all round the timber, 25mm and 45mm from one end to mark the position of the mortise, and 70mm from the same end to mark the length of the fence.

2. Use a mortise gauge to mark a 20mm-wide mortise in the centre of the face side. Mark both sides. If you have only a marking gauge set it first to 20mm and then to 40mm.

3. Mark the waste.

POINTS FOR EMPHASIS

o   It is important to start with an oversized piece of wood so that the mortise can be marked out and cut accurately.
o   All marking out must be done from the face side or the face edge; otherwise the stem will not fit square into the stock.

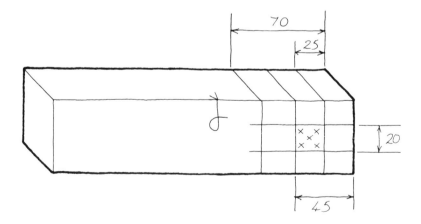

14   *Mortise gauge*

DEMO 2   Cutting the mortise

Why   So that the stem will fit the mortise.

Materials   Workpiece from the last demonstration.

Tools   12mm chisel; mallet or hammer.

ACTIONS

1. Place the chisel 2mm from the pencil line with the bevel facing the middle
    of the joint. Drive the chisel straight down. Replace the chisel and remove
    a small piece of waste from behind the first cut. When you reach the centre
    of the mortise, turn the chisel round and start from the other pencil line.
    Cut halfway through from one side. Turn the workpiece over and finish
    cutting from the other side.

2. Cut right through, then clean all four sides of the mortise up to the marks.
    Check that the insides of the joint are straight; you can do this with the
    edge of a chisel.

POINTS FOR EMPHASIS

o The chisel must be used across the grain to cut the bulk of the waste.
o Leave 1mm or 2mm all round the mortise to be cleaned up when the joint
   has been cut right through.

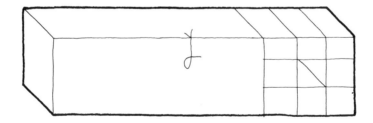

Fitting the stem

Why   So that the stem can slide through the stock.

Materials   One piece of hardwood 200 × 22 × 22mm; workpiece from
               the last demonstration.

Tools   Jack plane; pencil, marking gauge.

ACTIONS

1. Measure all the sides of the mortise on both sides of the fence; it should be
   20mm square but 1mm error either way is acceptable.

2. Gauge the piece for the stem as close as possible to the largest side of the
   mortise.

3. Carefully plane the first side of the stem down to the gauge lines. When
   you get close to the line, test the corners in the mortise. Take one shaving
   at a time and fit the corners into the stock. When all four corners of the
   stem fit into the mortise, mark the stem and the fence with an 'X', as in the
   drawing.

4. Now measure, gauge and plane the second side of the stem in the same
   way, until it fits right into the mortise.

POINTS FOR EMPHASIS

o Take one shaving at a time before trying to fit the stem into the stock.
o The stock should be tight enough not to fall off the stem, and loose enough
   to slide easily.

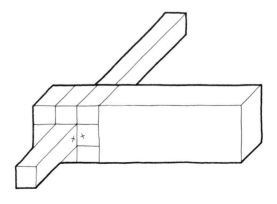

16   *Mortise gauge*

DEMO 4   Cutting the housing for the wedge

Why   So that the wedge can be fitted into the stock.

Materials   The stock of the gauge with finished mortise.

Tools   Try-square; marking gauge; tape measure; pencil; 6mm chisel; mallet or hammer.

ACTIONS

1. On one side of the stock, square a line 10mm from the mortise towards the end of the stock. On the other side, square a line 5mm from the mortise towards the same end.

2. Use a mortise gauge to mark the sides of the housing on both sides of the stock. It should be 6mm wide and centred in the side the mortise. If you have only a marking gauge, set it first to 27mm and then to 33mm, gauging from the face side.

3. Mark the waste.

4. Use a 6mm chisel and a mallet or hammer to cut the housing. From both sides, chisel down at an angle to meet in the middle of the mortise.

5. Turn the fence over so that the big side of the housing is on top; carefully cut until the end of the housing is straight and meets the pencil lines on both sides.

POINTS FOR EMPHASIS

o   The different dimensions allow for the taper in the wedge.

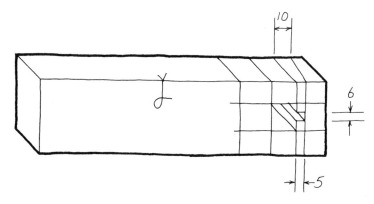

Mortise gauge 17

DEMO 5   Making the wedge

Why   The wedge fixes the stock and the stem together.

Materials   One piece of hardwood 100 × 15 × 6mm.

Tools   Try-square; tape measure; pencil; tenon-saw; 12mm chisel.

ACTIONS

1. Draw a diagonal line from one corner of the workpiece to 3mm above the other corner.

2. Mark a small knob 10mm from the small end.

3. Use a tenon-saw to remove the bulk of the waste. Place the wedge on a bench hook to cut down behind the knob.

4. Carefully pare the wedge down, holding it against the stop of the bench hook.

5. Round off the ends with a chisel and some sandpaper.

6. Fit the wedge into the housing of the stock and then push the stem into the mortise. Push the wedge tight with your thumb and check that there are no gaps between it and the stock.

POINTS FOR EMPHASIS

o   The knob will prevent the wedge falling out of the stock.

18 *Mortise gauge*

DEMO 6   Shaping the stock

Why   So that the gauge is comfortable to hold.

Materials   Workpieces from the last demonstration; sandpaper.

Tools   Tenon-saw; large tin; pencil; 25mm chisel; sandpaper.

ACTIONS

1. Using a tin or similar object of about 100mm diameter, mark a radius on both ends and sides of the stock.

2. Make four angled cuts with a tenon-saw as close to the curved line as possible.

3. Place the stock on a smooth piece of scrap timber; using a sharp chisel, pare the end grain to form an even curve.

4. Use some sandpaper to smooth the curve and round off the corners to make it feel comfortable in your hand.

POINTS FOR EMPHASIS

o   The appearance of the gauge will be improved if both curves are even.

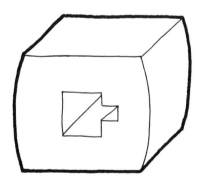

DEMO 7   Fitting the spurs

Why

So that the gauge can be used as a marking gauge or to mark 6mm and 10mm mortises.

Materials

Workpieces from the last demonstration; five 25mm wire nails.

Tools

Try-square; tape measure; pencil; hammer; hacksaw or pincers; saw file.

ACTIONS

1. Square a line all round the stem 30mm from one end. This marks the position of all the pins nearest the fence.

2. Mark out the stock as shown in the drawing.

3. Gauge the middle of each line.

4. Take the 25mm nails and blunt the ends with a hammer. Hammer the nails three-quarters of the way in, exactly where the lines cross.

5. Cut the heads of the nails off, leaving about 5mm sticking out from the stem.

6. Sharpen each nail into a point with a saw file.

POINTS FOR EMPHASIS

o Blunting the ends of the nails should prevent them from splitting the stem as they are driven in.

o It is important that each pair of spurs is the same height so that they both mark equally.

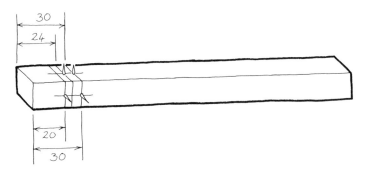

DEMO 8   Using the gauge

Why   So that you can gauge the width and thickness of timber, and
                   mark 6mm and 10mm mortises.

Materials   Scrap timber, planed face side and face edge.

Tools   Finished mortise gauge; tape measure.

ACTIONS

1. Set the fence to the required position, either by using a ruler or by trial and
   error, setting it from both sides of a piece of timber.

2. Tighten the wedge by tapping the big end gently on the edge of your
   bench.

3. Test the setting. Any minor adjustments can be made by tapping the end
   of the stem gently on the bench. Test the setting once more before you use
   the gauge.

4. To loosen the fence simply tap the small end of the wedge against the edge
   of your bench.

BOW-SAW

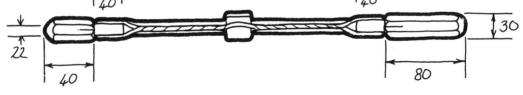

22   Bow-saw

Objective

At the end of this session each participant will have made a bow-saw.

Previous knowledge assumed

Competence in: preparing timber, marking out and cutting mortise and tenon joints.

Tools required

Try-square   Tenon-saw
Pencil   Wheel brace
Steel rule or tape measure   3mm drill bit
Jack plane   Carpenters' brace
Marking gauge   16mm auger bit
6mm chisel   Rasp or file
25mm chisel   Saw set
Mallet   Saw file

Common problems

Drilling the holes for the handles out of square
Making the dowels on the handles too small
Not sharpening and setting the teeth correctly

Cutting list

The instructor and each student need to prepare hardwood timber to the following dimensions (mm):

ITEM	QUANTITY	MATERIAL	L	W	T
Style	2	Hardwood	400	40	22
Rail	1	Hardwood	350	40	22
Handles	1	Hardwood	200	30	30
Twisting slat	1	Hardwood	180	20	6

Also needed

One metre thick string
Two 50mm nails
Suitable blade 440mm long

Introduction

Time   Two days.

What   In this session we are going to make a bow-saw.

Why   A bow-saw can be used for all kinds of work. If it is fitted
              with a narrow blade it can be used for cutting curves; when
              fitted with a wide blade it can be used to cut tenons and even
              rip timber to width. Tenon-saws and rip-saws are often quite
              expensive, so if suitable blades can be obtained bow-saws are
              a cheaper option. The best sources for blades are butchers'
              hacksaws or old band-saw blades.

How   The session will be made up of a series of demonstrations.
              Each step will be demonstrated two or three times. I will ask
              some questions to check that the demonstration was clear,
              then you will practise the same operation. We will wait until
              everyone is finished before the next step is demonstrated.

This is the bow-saw we are going to make. [SHOW TOOL TO TRAINEES]
You use it like this.

These are the parts.

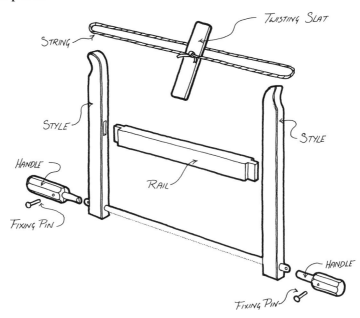

DEMO 1   Marking out the frame

Why   So that the joints in the frames can be cut.

Materials Two pieces of 400 × 40 × 22mm hardwood; one piece 350 × 40 × 22mm.

Tools   Try-square; mortise or marking gauge; tape measure; pencil.

ACTIONS

1. Square a line all round both styles, 25mm from one end, to mark the position of the holes for the handles. Square lines on the face edges, 180mm and 220mm from the same end, to mark the position of the mortises.

2. Gauge the the centre of the holes at the bottom of the styles, on both edges. Use a mortise gauge to gauge a 6mm mortise in the middle of both styles, on the face edge. If you have only have a marking gauge set it first to 8mm and then to 14mm.

3. Square lines all round the rail, 15mm from each end, to mark the length of the tenons. Use the same gauge settings to mark the cheeks of the tenons.

POINTS FOR EMPHASIS

o   All marking out must be done from the face side or the face edge.

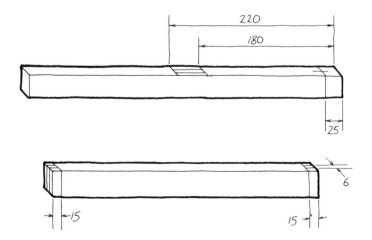

DEMO 2   Cutting the joints in the frame

Why   So that the frame can be assembled.

Materials   Workpieces from the last demonstration.

Tools   Carpenters' brace; 16mm auger bit; 6mm mortise chisel; mallet or hammer; tenon-saw.

ACTIONS

1. Take the styles and drill a 16mm hole right through. To bore this hole accurately, drill halfway through from one side, turn the piece over and drill to meet the first hole from the other side.

2. Use a 6mm mortise chisel and a mallet or hammer to cut the mortises to a depth of 20mm.

3. Cut the tenons by placing the rail in the vice at an angle pointing away from you. Position the tenon-saw on the waste side of the gauge line, and saw horizontally down to the pencil line. Saw down both sides of the tenon. Turn the stock round and replace vertically in the vice to finish the cut. The kerf of the first cut will guide the saw at the far side.

4. Saw the shoulders of the tenon and fit the joint.

POINTS FOR EMPHASIS

o   Ask someone to check that the drill is square.
o   Saw on the waste side of the line.
o   This method of sawing the tenon allows you to see both edges as they are being sawn. The kerf of the first cut will guide the saw at the far side.
o   The joints must not be glued because the styles pivot slightly around the rail as the string is tightened.

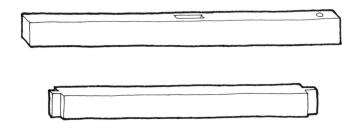

DEMO 3   Shaping the styles

Why   The top of each style should have a small hollow to keep the string in place when it is loose.

Materials   Workpieces from the last demonstration.

Tools   Tenon-saw; 25mm chisel; pencil; small tin; mallet or hammer.

ACTIONS

1.   On the opposite side to the mortise, thumb-gauge a line at the top of the styles, 10mm from the edge.

2.   Draw around a small tin which should be positioned so that the radius meets the top corner and touches the 10mm line. Repeat this on the top of both styles, on both sides.

3.   Use a tenon-saw to make a series of cuts down to the radius. This helps to remove the waste cleanly.

4.   Chisel out the bottom of the curve with a 25mm chisel. Work from both sides so that you are not cutting against the grain.

5.   To finish off, pare a slight radius on the inside edge of each style.

POINTS FOR EMPHASIS

○   A sharp chisel will be needed.
○   When paring the hollow, the bevel of the chisel should be face down and used to control the cut.
○   Place the style on a scrap piece of timber to pare the end grain.

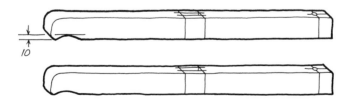

Bow-saw   27

DEMO 4   Marking out the handles

Why   So that the pins that hold the blade in position can be cut.

Materials   One piece of 200 × 30 × 30mm hardwood. Both handles will
                     be made from this piece of timber.

Tools   Marking gauge; tape measure; try-square; pencil.

ACTIONS

1. Square a line all round, 40mm from both ends, to mark the length of the
    pins. Square another line all round 80mm from one end to mark the length
    of the front and back handles.

2. Set a mortise gauge to mark the chamfers and a 16mm-wide pin in the
    centre of the handle. Gauge all four sides as well as the end grain. If you
    have only have a marking gauge, set it first to 7mm and then to 23mm.

POINTS FOR EMPHASIS

o   All marking out must be done from the face side or the face edge.

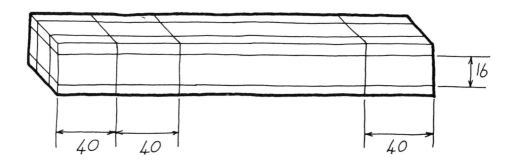

DEMO 5 Cutting the pins in the handles

Why　　　　So that the pins can pass through the styles.

Materials　　Workpiece from the last demonstration.

Tools　　　Tenon-saw; 25mm chisel; file or rasp.

ACTIONS

1. Cut the pins by placing the handle in the vice at an angle pointing away from you. Position the tenon-saw on the waste side of the gauge line and saw horizontally down to the pencil line. Saw down both sides of the pin.

2. Turn the handle round and replace it vertically in the vice to finish the cut. The kerf of the first cut will guide the saw at the far side. Repeat at both ends of the handle.

3. Saw the shoulders, taking care not to cut below the gauge lines as this will weaken the pins considerably.

4. Use a chisel to take off the corners of the pins and then file them into dowels.

5. Fit the pins into the styles.

6. Plane the edges of the handles down to the gauge lines.

POINTS FOR EMPHASIS

○ Saw on the waste side of the line.
○ Do not make the pins too small as they may become weak.

DEMO 6   Slitting and drilling the handle

Why   So that the blade can be fitted.

Materials   Workpiece from the last demonstration.

Tools   Tape-measure or ruler; pencil; tenon-saw; wheel brace; 3mm
                   bit; sandpaper; chisel.

ACTIONS

1. Mark a point 20mm from both shoulders towards the middle on both sides
    of the handle. This marks the length of the saw kerf into which the blade
    will fit.

2. From both shoulders, this time on the adjacent edges, mark a point 10mm
    towards the middle. This marks the position of the holes for the fixing pins.

3. Saw down the centre of the pin to the second pencil mark.

4. At the first pencil mark, drill a 3mm hole right through the handle.

5. Saw the two handles apart.

6. Use a chisel and sandpaper to round off the ends.

POINTS FOR EMPHASIS

o Saw the pin carefully, judging the centres by eye.
o Ask someone to check that the drill is square.

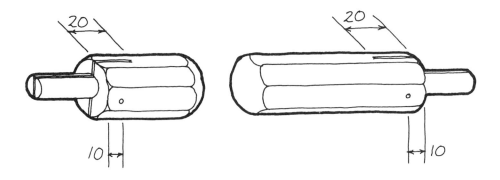

DEMO 7   Chamfering the frame

Why   To prevent splinters and make the saw comfortable to hold.

Materials   The two styles and the rail.

Tools   Jack plane; chisel; pencil.

ACTIONS

1. Thumb-gauge pencil lines 4mm from each edge on all four sides. Mark the stopped chamfers where the rail meets the style.

2. Plane down to the pencil lines on the straight edges, and use a chisel to work the curved and the stopped chamfers.

POINTS FOR EMPHASIS

o Even chamfers will improve the appearance of the saw.

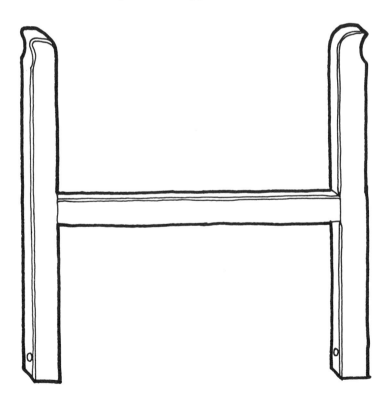

DEMO 8 Fitting the blade

Why   So that the blade can be fitted securely to the frame.

Materials   One 440mm length of blade; the two handles; the frame.

Tools   Grinding wheel or file; wheel brace; 3mm bit (a saw file and saw set may also be needed).

ACTIONS

1. Cut a piece of blade to 440mm in length. If necessary, file or grind the first 60mm of each end to 16mm in width, so that the blade fits through the holes in the styles.

2. Centre punch and drill a 3mm diameter hole 10mm from each end.

3. If the blade has less than eight points per inch, the teeth will have to be recut. This can be done by first filing or grinding off half of each tooth, then cutting an extra tooth in the flat thus formed.

POINTS FOR EMPHASIS

o Blades for curved work should be less than 12mm wide. A blade to be used for cutting joints or ripping should be at least 25mm wide.
o The blade should be sharpened like a cross-cut saw, with a pitch of about 80 degrees.

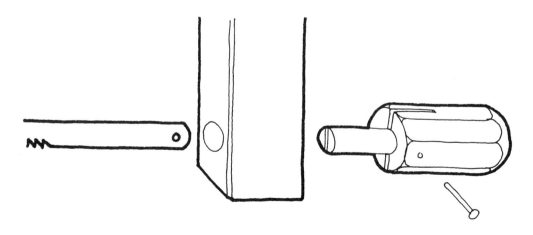

DEMO 9 Assembling the saw

Materials   The three pieces of the frame; the two handles; one piece of nylon string 1m long; one blade; two 50mm nails; one piece of $180 \times 20 \times 6$mm hardwood (twisting slat).

Tools   Hacksaw.

ACTIONS

1. Make the fixing pins by cutting two 50mm nails down to 30mm in length, leaving the heads on.

2. Push the blade through the holes in the styles and fit the rail.

3. Insert the handles (the teeth should point towards the small handle) and secure the blade with the fixing pins.

4. Wind a length of string two or three times around the top of the frame and tie it tightly. Push the slat into the loop of string and twist it several times until the blade is tensioned. Then let the twisting slat rest against the rail. The saw is now ready to use.

POINTS FOR EMPHASIS

○ Applying the correct tension on the blade is a skill gained with experience. If it is too loose the blade will twist; if it is too tight it may break the handles.

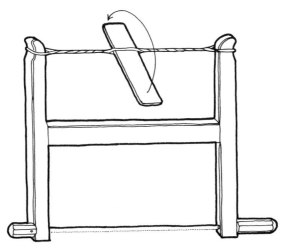

DEMO 10   Using the bow-saw

Why   So you will be able to use the saw for ripping, cross-cutting
                     and cutting curves.

Materials   One piece of scrap timber, about $400 \times 150 \times 20$mm.

Tools   Completed bow-saw; bench hook.

ACTIONS

1. To cross-cut timber on a bench hook, turn the handles until the blade is in
    line with the frame at both ends. Hold the work against a bench hook and
    saw as if using a tenon-saw.

2. To rip timber held in a vice the frame has to be held at a slight angle while
    the blade cuts vertically.

POINTS FOR EMPHASIS

○   In all cases it is important that the blade is not twisted. When tackling
    curved work a narrow blade needs to be fitted, so that where necessary the
    blade can be turned to saw horizontally or vertically while the frame is held
    upright.
○   When ripping or cross-cutting, a wide blade needs to be fitted.

SASH CLAMP

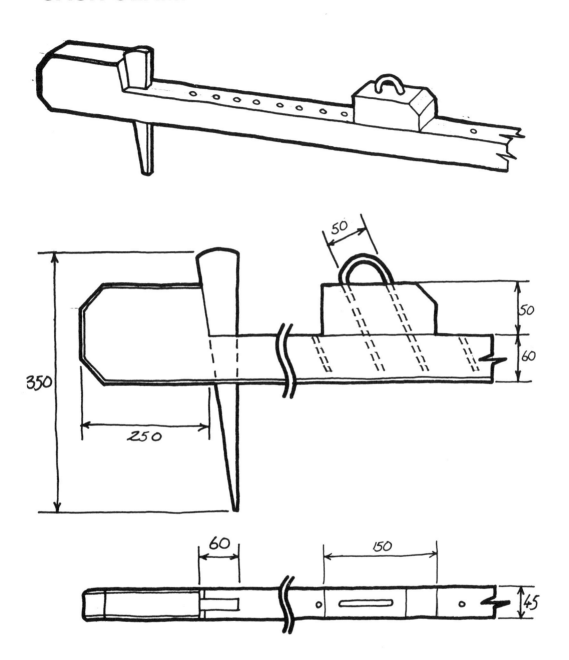

Objective

At the end of this session each participant will have made a sash clamp.

Previous knowledge assumed

Competence in: preparing timber, marking out and cutting through mortises.

Tools required

Try-square
Pencil
Steel rule or tape measure
Marking gauge
Jack plane
Tenon-saw
12mm chisel
25mm chisel
Mallet
Carpenters' brace
12mm auger bit

Common problems

Cutting the angled mortise
Fitting the wedge
Bending the fixing pins

Cutting list

The instructor and each student need to prepare hardwood timber to the following dimensions (mm):

ITEM	QUANTITY	MATERIAL	L	W	T
Stock	1	Hardwood	1500	120	45
Shoe	1	Hardwood	150	50	45
Wedge	1	Hardwood	420	60	15

Also needed

One piece of 12mm diameter mild steel rod, 360mm long

Introduction

Time   One day.

What   In this session we are going to make a simple wooden sash clamp.

Why   Sash clamps are essential tools for clamping up joints in all kinds of joinery work. Steel clamps are expensive, while wooden clamps can be made at a fraction of the cost.

How   The session will be made up of a series of demonstrations. Each step will be demonstrated two or three times. I will ask some questions to check that the demonstration was clear, then you will practise the same operation. We will wait until everyone is finished before the next step is demonstrated.

       From the timber supplied you will be able to make two clamps, so during the first two demonstrations you will need to work in pairs.

This is the clamp we will make. [SHOW TOOL TO TRAINEES] It works like this.

These are the parts.

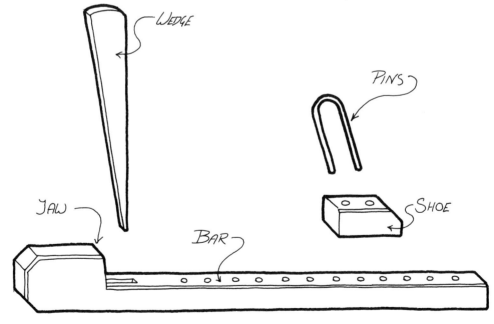

DEMO 1   Marking out the stock

Why   So that the stocks of the clamps can be cut.

Materials   One piece of hardwood 1500 × 120 × 45mm (a piece of timber this size will produce two clamps with a capacity of 1m).

Tools   Marking gauge; tape measure; try-square; pencil.

ACTIONS

1. Gauge a centre line down both sides.

2. Square lines all round, 250mm and 310mm from both ends. Mark the angled jaws by squaring a line on the edges of both ends, 10mm to the left of the 250mm marks. Draw diagonal lines to mark the jaws.

3. Mark the waste as shown in the drawing.

POINTS FOR EMPHASIS

o All marking out must be done from the face side or the face edge.
o The angled lines marked for the jaws must be parallel.
o Removing the waste as marked will allow you to rip the two clamps apart.

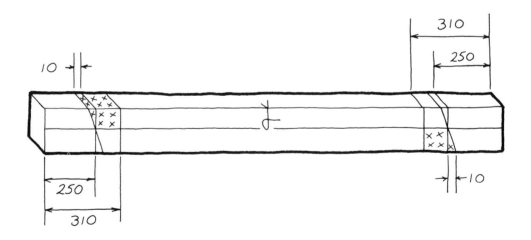

DEMO 2 Sawing the two clamps apart

Why   So that both clamps can be mortised and drilled.

Materials   Workpiece from last demonstration.

Tools   Tenon-saw; 25mm chisel; mallet or hammer; ripsaw.

ACTIONS

1. Use a tenon-saw to cut the angled jaw and the end of the bar from both ends of the stock. Make two or three saw cuts in the waste to make chiselling easier.

2. Cut out the waste with a 25mm chisel and a mallet or hammer. Check that the bottom of the housing is straight.

3. Fit the end of a small handsaw into the housing and begin ripping down the centre line.

4. Plane the sawn edges smooth and square; clean up the edge close to the jaw by paring away the waste with a chisel.

POINTS FOR EMPHASIS

o   When ripping down the centre line, keep checking the back of the stock to make sure the saw is square.

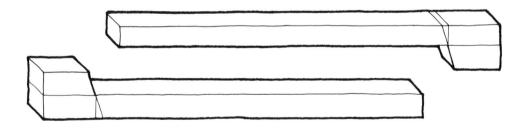

Sash clamp   39

DEMO 3   Cutting the mortise for the wedge

Why   So that the wedge can pass through the stock.

Materials   Workpiece from last demonstration.

Tools   Marking gauge; tape measure; try-square; pencil; 12mm chisel; mallet or hammer.

ACTIONS

1. Square a line all round the stock, 310mm from the end of the jaw, to mark the end of the through mortise.

2. Use a mortise gauge to mark a 15mm mortise in the centre of the stock or use a marking gauge set at 15mm to gauge from both sides.

3. Chop out the waste with a mortise chisel. Cut halfway through from one side, turn the stock over and finish the mortise from the other side.

POINTS FOR EMPHASIS

o   It is important that the end of the mortise follows the angle of the jaw. Use a straight edge to test this.

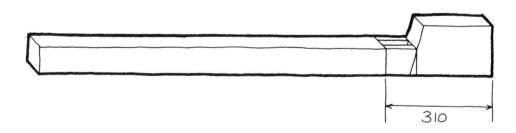

DEMO 4   Making the wedge

Why   The wedge will act like the screw thread in a manufactured clamp to force the joint in the workpieces together.

Materials   One piece of hardwood $420 \times 60 \times 15$mm.

Tools   Pencil; straight edge; ripsaw; tenon-saw; jack plane; try-square.

ACTIONS

1. Mark a diagonal line from one corner to the other.

2. Use a handsaw to rip down the centre of the line, and plane the sawn edge straight and square.

3. Mark a radius at the top of the wedge with a pencil and a tin, or similar object, about 150mm in diameter.

4. Cut and smooth the radius down to the pencil line, and chamfer the top edges.

5. Saw off about 10mm from the small end.

6. Fit the wedge into the stock.

POINTS FOR EMPHASIS

o The chamfered radius at the top of the wedge prevents the wedge from splitting when struck with a hammer.

DEMO 5   Making the shoe

Why   When fixed to the stock the shoe will act against the wedge
                  to force the two parts of the joint together.

Materials   One piece of hardwood 150 × 50 × 45mm.

Tools   Try-square; marking gauge; tape measure; pencil; carpen-
                  ters' brace; 12mm auger bit.

ACTIONS

1. Square lines all round 50mm from each end. On the face edge, square lines
    20mm to the left of the first two lines and mark the diagonals. This marks
    the angled holes for the pins.

2. Use a marking gauge to gauge a centre line on the top and bottom of the
    shoe.

3. Clamp the shoe in a vice so that the holes can be drilled vertically.

4. Drill both holes halfway through. Turn the shoe over and clamp in the vice
    in the same way. Drill to meet the first holes from the other side.

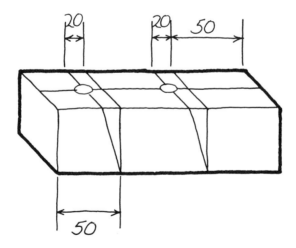

DEMO 6   Forming the pins

Why   The pins hold the shoe firmly in position.

Materials   One piece of 12mm diameter steel rod, 360mm long.

Tools   Hacksaw; file; tape measure; length of steel pipe.

ACTIONS

1. Take the length of 12mm mild steel rod and make two marks, 150mm from
    each end.

2. Clamp it between two blocks in a vice so that the first mark is level with
    the top of the bench. Take a piece of pipe, placing it over the rod about
    20mm from the top of the bench, and bend it through half a right angle.

3. Move the pipe 20mm up the tube and bend the rod to form a right angle.

4. Continue this process until the two ends of the rod are parallel, and 50mm
    apart.

5. Make any final adjustments with a hammer.

6. Fit the pins into the shoe.

POINTS FOR EMPHASIS

o Use scrap wood to avoid damaging the jaws of the vice.
o The pipe acts as a lever and helps to control the bending.

DEMO 7   Drilling the stock

Why   So that the fixing pins can be fitted into the stock.

Materials   Workpiece from last demonstration; the stock; the shoe.

Tools   Carpenters' brace; 12mm auger bit; 'G' clamp.

ACTIONS

1. Clamp the shoe in position at the end of the bar, making sure that the holes for the pins point towards the back of the bar and the sides of the shoe are flush with the sides of the bar.

2. Take a carpenters' brace and a 12mm auger bit. Make a mark on the drill 100mm from the end, drill through both holes in the shoe and into the bar. Stop when you reach the mark on the bit.

3. Move the shoe up the bar and push one side of the fixing pin through the hole at the back of the shoe and into the second hole in the bar. Clamp the shoe in position and drill until you reach the mark on the auger bit.

4. Continue drilling these regularly-spaced holes up to a distance of 200mm from the jaw.

5. Fit both pins into the shoe and check that it will fit into each of the holes.

POINTS FOR EMPHASIS

o Make sure the side of the shoe is flush with the side of the stock before drilling each hole.

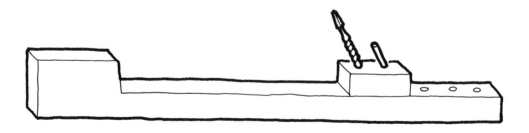

44   *Sash clamp*

DEMO 8   Chamfering the edges

Why   So that the tool is comfortable to use.

Materials   Finished stock and shoe.

Tools   Pencil; ruler; tenon-saw; 25mm chisel; jack plane.

ACTIONS

1. Mark off two 30mm × 30mm mitres at the front of the stock, and a 20mm × 20mm mitre at the back of the shoe.

2. Cut the mitres with a tenon-saw.

3. Thumb-gauge pencil lines 4mm from each edge on all sides of the stock.

4. Thumb-gauge pencil lines 4mm from the top edges of the shoe.

5. Plane the chamfers down to the pencil lines.

POINTS FOR EMPHASIS

o   The appearance of the clamp will be improved if the chamfers are even.

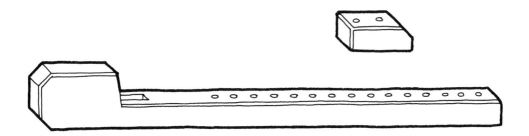

DEMO 9   Using the sash clamp

Why   So that you can clamp up frames.

Materials   Completed sash clamp; sample frame.

Tools   Mallet.

ACTIONS

1. Place the clamps on a workbench so that the mortises are clear of the side; this gives room for the wedges to move.

2. Place the frame on the clamps.

3. Position the shoes as close to the frame as possible, allowing some space for the wedge.

4. Push the wedge into the mortise and drive it down with a mallet. As the wedge is driven home the joints will close up. Check that the frame is lying flat on the bars.

5. To loosen the clamp simply hit the bottom of the wedges.

6. Remember to prevent the frame from sticking to the clamp by covering it with paper below the glue lines.

BENCH CLAMP

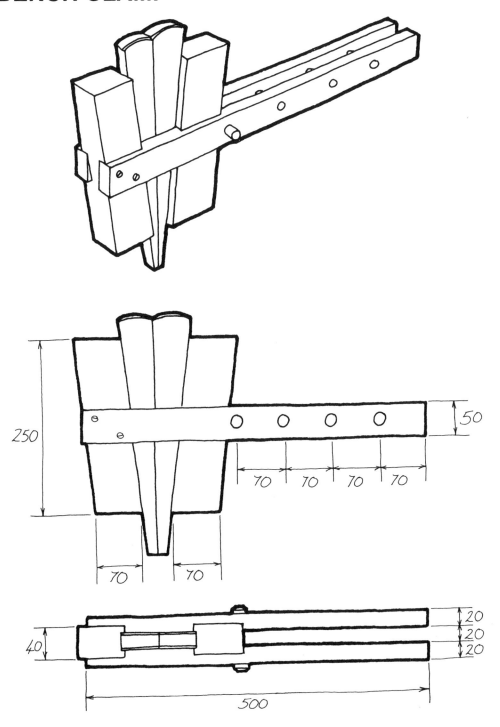

Objective

At the end of this session each participant will have made a bench clamp.

Previous knowledge assumed

Competence in: preparing timber, marking out and cutting housing joints.

Tools required

Try-square
Pencil
Steel rule or tape measure
Jack plane
Marking gauge
25mm chisel
Mallet or hammer

Tenon-saw
Carpenter's brace
20mm auger bit
Wheel brace
3mm and 5mm twist bits
Screwdriver

Common problems

Cutting the housings too big
Screwing the bars to the jaw
Fitting the wedges

Cutting list

The instructor and students need to prepare hardwood to the following dimensions (mm):

ITEM	QUANTITY	MATERIAL	L	W	T
Jaws	1	Hardwood	510	70	40
Bars	2	Hardwood	500	50	20
Wedges	1	Hardwood	320	50	20
Fixing pin	1	Hardwood	120	20	20

Also needed

Four 30mm wood-screws
PVA wood glue

Introduction

Time   One day.

What   In this session we are all going to make a simple bench clamp.

Why   Although not as compact as a 'G' clamp, the tool described here can be used to do the same sort of work. It is easily made in a few hours and can be used to clamp timber to the bench while ripping and mortising, or to clamp small pieces together during assembly.

How   The session will be made up of a series of demonstrations. Each step will be demonstrated two or three times. I will ask some questions to check that the demonstration was clear, then you will practise the same operation. We will wait until everyone is finished before the next step is demonstrated.

This is the bench clamp we are going to make. [SHOW TOOL TO TRAINEES] It works like this.

These are the parts.

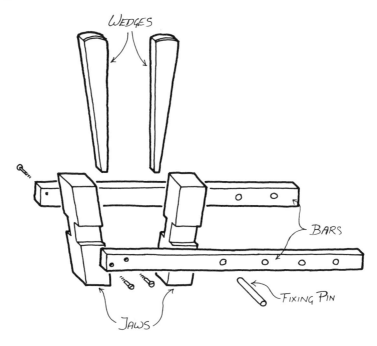

Bench clamp 49

DEMO 1   Marking out the jaw

Why   So that the housings in the jaws can be cut.

Materials   One piece of hardwood 510 × 70 × 40mm (both jaws will be
                 made from this piece of timber).

Tools   Try-square; marking gauge; pencil; tape measure.

ACTIONS

1. Square lines across the face edge 100mm, 150mm, 250mm, 350mm, 400mm
    and 500mm from one end, leaving 10mm extra. On the opposite edge but
    from the same end, square lines across 10mm, 110mm, 160mm, 260mm,
    360mm, 410mm and 510mm. Continue these lines round the sides to mark
    the angled housings in the jaws.

2. To mark the depth of the housing set a mortise gauge to mark two lines
    20mm apart, in the centre of the jaw, on both edges. If you have only a
    marking gauge, set it first to 10mm and then to 30mm, and gauge from the
    face side.

3. Mark the waste.

POINTS FOR EMPHASIS

o   All marking out must be done from the face side or the face edge.

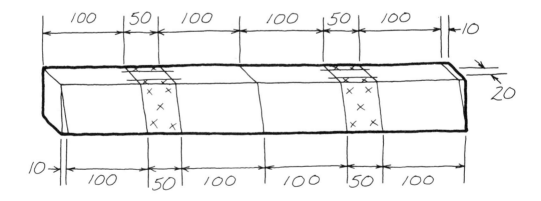

50   *Bench clamp*

DEMO 2   Cutting the housing joints

Why   So that the bars can be fitted to the jaws.

Materials   Workpiece from the last demonstration.

Tools   Tenon-saw; 25mm chisel; mallet or hammer.

ACTIONS

1. Saw down the sides of the housing with a tenon-saw, on the waste side of the pencil marks. Make two or three cuts down to the gauge line.

2. Remove the waste with a wide chisel, checking the bottom of the joint with a straight edge.

3. All four housings should be cut in the same way.

4. Cut the two jaws apart along the centre line.

5. Saw off the angled ends.

6. Finally, lightly chamfer all the edges with a plane.

POINTS FOR EMPHASIS

○ Saw down the waste side of the pencil lines.
○ Do not saw below the gauge lines.
○ Making two or three saw cuts in the waste helps when chopping out the housing.

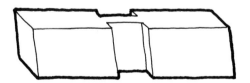 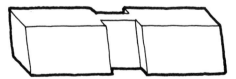

DEMO 3   Marking out the bars

Why   So that the holes in the bars can be drilled.

Materials   Two pieces of hardwood 500 × 50 × 20mm.

Tools   Try-square; marking gauge; pencil; tape measure.

ACTIONS

1. Holding or clamping the two pieces together, square four lines across the edges at 70mm intervals. These mark the position of the holes for the fixing pin.

2. From the other end, square lines across 20mm and 60mm to mark the position of the screws.

3. Square these lines all round the bars.

4. Set a marking gauge to half the width of the bars and gauge the centre of the holes for the fixing pins. Gauge both sides of both pieces.

5. Set a marking gauge to 15mm and gauge the centre of the screw holes from both sides.

POINTS FOR EMPHASIS

o   Holding or clamping the two parts together allows them to be marked out in equal measures.

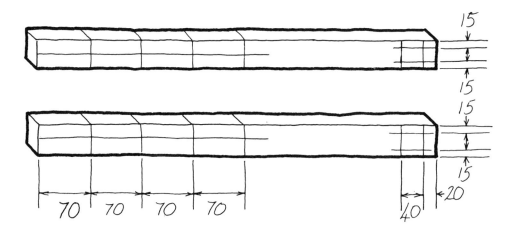

52   *Bench clamp*

DEMO 4   Drilling the bars

Why   The bars are drilled in the back to take the fixing pin, and in
                     the front to take the wood screws that fix the bars to the
                     jaws.

Materials   Workpieces from the last demonstration.

Tools   Carpenters' brace; 20mm auger bit; wheel brace; 4mm twist
                     bit (countersink bit if available).

ACTIONS

1. Drill four 20mm holes in the back of each bar, remembering to drill
   halfway through on both sides.

2. Drill two 4mm clearance holes right through each bar for the wood-screws.

3. Countersink the screw holes.

POINTS FOR EMPHASIS

o   Ask someone to check that the drill is square.
o   The holes for the screws should be at diagonals from each other so that the
    screws do not meet when the clamp is being assembled.

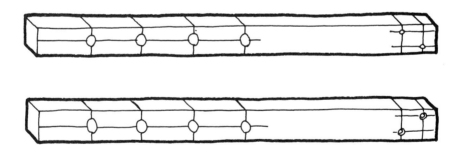

DEMO 5 Making the fixing pin

Why   The fixing pin holds the back jaw in position.

Materials   One piece of hardwood 120 × 20 × 20mm.

Tools   Smoothing plane.

ACTIONS

1. Chamfer the edges to form an octagonal section with a small plane.

2. Shave off the corners of the octagon to form a dowel and fit it into the bars.

3. Fit the fixing pin into the bars.

POINTS FOR EMPHASIS

o Whenever accurate dowels need to be prepared start with a piece of timber that is the same width and thickness as the diameter of the dowel required.

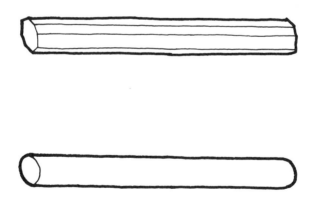

DEMO 6   Assembling the clamp

Why   The bars must be fixed securely to the front jaw to withstand
                 the force of the wedges.

Materials   Four 30mm wood-screws; PVA wood glue.

Tools   Wheel brace; 3mm twist bit; screwdriver.

ACTIONS

1. Fit the bars into the housing joint in one of the jaws. These joints should be
    a tight fit.

2. Drill four 3mm pilot holes through the bars and into the jaw.

3. Screw the bars tightly to the jaw. Glue can be used but it is not essential.

4. Fit the adjustable jaw onto the back of the clamp. It should slide easily
    along the bars but stay at a constant angle.

POINTS FOR EMPHASIS

○   Drilling the correct size of pilot hole is essential, particularly in hardwoods.

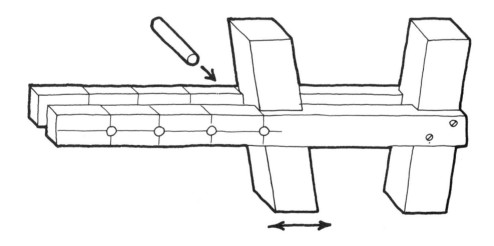

DEMO 7   Making the wedges

Why   The wedges will act like the screw thread in a manufactured
                 clamp to force the joint in the workpieces together.

Materials   One piece of hardwood 320 × 50 × 20mm.

Tools   Straight edge; pencil; ripsaw; jack plane; tenon-saw.

ACTIONS

1. Mark a diagonal line from one corner to the other.

2. Use a handsaw to rip down the centre of the line, and plane the sawn edge
    straight and square.

3. Mark a radius at the top of the wedge with a pencil and a tin (or similar
    object) about 150mm in diameter.

4. Cut and smooth the radius down to the pencil line and chamfer the top
    edges. This will prevent the wedge from splitting when it is struck with a
    hammer.

5. Saw off about 10mm from the small end.

6. Fit the wedges into the clamp, making sure that they meet along the whole
    of their length.

POINTS FOR EMPHASIS

○   If the clamp is to work well the wedges must fit tightly between the jaws.

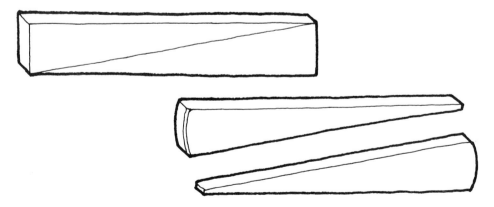

56   *Bench clamp*

DEMO 8 Using the clamp

Why   So that workpieces can be clamped to the bench.

Materials   The finished bench clamp; some pieces of scrap timber.

Tools   Mallet.

ACTIONS

1. Position the adjustable jaw so that the pieces to be held will fit between the jaws of the clamp; insert the fixing pin.

2. Push the wedges through the bars, between the timber to be clamped and the jaws.

3. To tighten the clamp, use a mallet to drive the wedges against the jaws.

4. To loosen the clamp, hit the back of the jaw or the thin end of the wedge with a mallet.

POINTS FOR EMPHASIS

o In order to prevent the clamp from sticking to your workpiece when gluing up a joint, place a piece of paper or a wood shaving under the glue line.

o If made slightly longer, clamps like these could be used for gluing up small frames or chairs.

Workshop lesson: Making planes

Objective

At the end of this session each participant will understand the function of each part of a woodworking plane.

Previous knowledge assumed

Basic understanding of how to use smoothing planes, jack planes, rebate planes and plough planes.

Teaching aids required

Smoothing plane
Jack plane
Rebate plane
Plough plane

Bench and vice
Scrap timber
Blackboard.

Introduction

All woodworking planes – plough planes, rebate planes and moulding planes as well as the jack and the smoothing plane – have a number of components in common, each of which must be understood if you are to make a plane that works well.

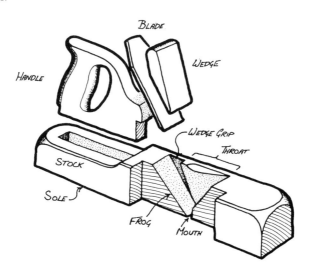

The sole

1. Unless the plane has been designed for planing curved work the sole must be straight and flat.

2. It is very difficult to produce a straight surface if the sole of the plane is twisted or bowed.

The mouth

1. The mouth of the plane is where the blade passes through the sole.

2. It should be as narrow as possible if the plane is to leave a smooth finish.

3. When downward pressure is applied to the plane, the front of the mouth helps to prevent the workpiece from splitting ahead of the cutting edge (see Figure 1). A large mouth allows the split to develop, and will leave a rough surface on cross-grained timber (see Figure 2).

Figure 1

Figure 2

The frog

1. The blade is held against the frog of the plane, which should be between 45 and 50 degrees to the sole.

2. It must be straight and flat. If the frog is curved outwards the cutting edge of the blade will not be supported, and the blade will chatter (see Figure 3).

Figure 3

The throat

1. Shavings leave the plane through the throat.

2. On a wooden jack or smoothing plane this is the opening at the top of the stock. On a rebate plane it is the recess at the side of the stock.

3. It is essential that this opening is large enough for the shavings to pass through easily, otherwise the plane will 'choke up' and require constant clearing.

4. A common fault is that the fixing device is placed too close to the front of the throat.

5. On all jack or smoothing planes the width of the throat should be 3mm wider than the width of the blade to allow it to be adjusted laterally.

The fixing mechanism

1. The blade must be held securely against the frog but the fixing mechanism should also allow a certain amount of adjustment.

2. There are three main methods, as illustrated.

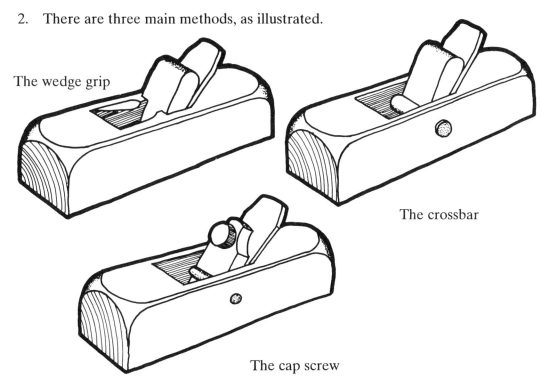

The wedge grip

The crossbar

The cap screw

The blade

1. This must be straight and flat to fit tightly onto the frog.

2. The cutting edge must be ground to an angle of 25 degrees; otherwise there will be no clearance behind the cutting angle when it is sharpened.

The hand hold

1. The plane must be comfortable to hold.

2. There should be no sharp edges on the upper surface.

3. If a handle is to be fitted it should fit the hand and not get in the way of the blade.

REBATE PLANE

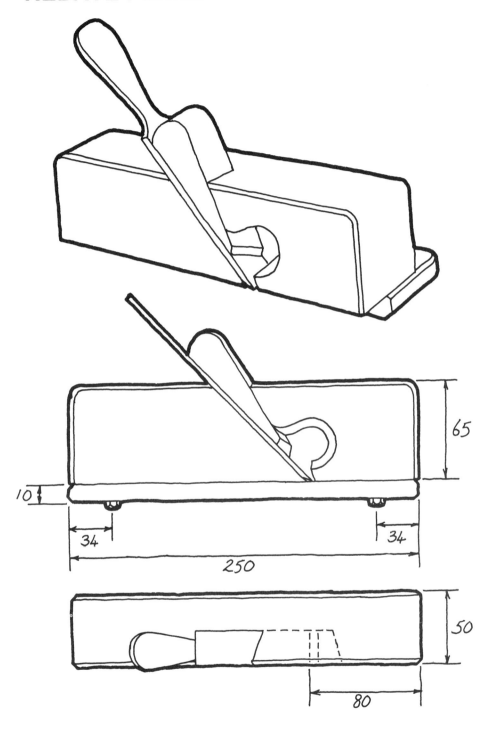

Objective

At the end of this session each participant will have made a rebate plane.

Previous knowledge assumed

Competence in: preparing timber, marking out and cutting mortise and tenon joints.

Tools required

Try-square
Pencil
Steel rule or tape measure
Jack plane
Marking gauge
6mm chisel
12mm chisel

25mm chisel
Mallet
Tenon-saw
Carpenter's brace
Wheel brace
6mm bit
12mm, 25mm auger bits

Common problems

Shaping the throat
Sawing the angle for the wedge
Fitting the wedge
Fitting the fence adjustment screws

Cutting list

The instructor and each student need to prepare hardwood timber to the following dimensions (mm):

ITEM	QUANTITY	MATERIAL	L	W	T
Stock	1	Hardwood	250	65	50
Fence	1	Hardwood	250	50	10
Wedge	1	Hardwood	150	25	25

Also needed

Suitable blade 25mm wide
Two 25 × 6mm nuts, bolts and washers

Introduction

<blockquote>

Time   One and a half days.

What   In this session we are going to make a simple wooden rebate plane.

Why   Rebate planes are used for making picture frames, letting panels into door frames and making wooden window casements. They are expensive and often unavailable in developing countries.

    Before you start, make sure you can obtain a suitable blade. A 25mm chisel can be used or a blade can be forged specially for the plane.

How   The session will be made up of a series of demonstrations. Each step will be demonstrated two or three times. I will ask some questions to check that the demonstration was clear, then you will practise the same operation. We will wait until everyone is finished before the next step is demonstrated.

</blockquote>

This is the rebate plane we will make. [SHOW TOOL TO TRAINEES] It works like this.

These are the parts.

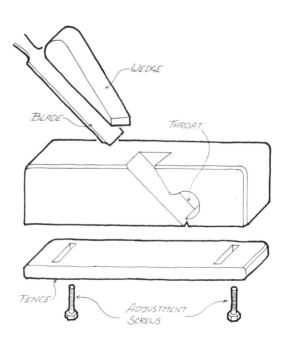

DEMO 1 **Marking out the stock**

Why   The plane must be accurately marked out if it is to work well.

Materials   One piece of hardwood 250 × 65 × 50mm.

Tools   Marking gauge; try-square; tape measure; pencil.

ACTIONS

1. Mark the front and the sole of the plane.

2. Mark out the frog and the angle for the wedge as shown in the drawing.

3. On the top, mark the width of the wedge at 25mm and draw a diagonal line to mark the wedge grip.

4. Gauge a line 25mm from the face edge to mark the depth of the frog on the top and bottom.

5. Mark the second angle for the wedge on the top and bottom by measuring 5mm towards the front and drawing two more diagonal lines.

6. Finally, gauge a line 25mm from the sole, across the first squared line, to mark the centre of the throat and mark the waste.

POINTS FOR EMPHASIS

o   All marking out must be done from the face side or the face edge.
o   There will be less friction if the grain rises towards the front.

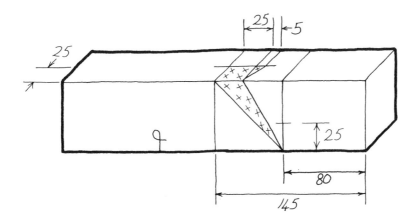

DEMO 2   Cutting the frog

Why   So that the blade and wedge can be fitted into the stock.

Materials   Workpiece from the last demonstration.

Tools   Tenon-saw; 6mm chisel; 12mm chisel; mallet.

ACTIONS

1. Clamp the stock on its side in the vice and saw the frog down to the gauge line on one side and to the far edge only. Turn the stock round in the vice to finish the cut. The first saw kerf will guide the second cut: this way you cut only the faces you can see.

2. Cut the compound angle that forms the wedge grip in the same way.

3. Remove the waste with a chisel, checking that the side of the throat is flat.

POINTS FOR EMPHASIS

o   Both saw cuts have to be done accurately: if the frog is not straight the blade will chatter. If the wedge grip is not straight the wedge will not tighten the blade properly.
o   Saw on the waste side of the pencil lines.
o   Do not saw below the gauge lines.

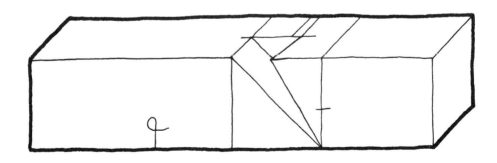

DEMO 3 — **Forming the throat**

Why   The throat allows the shavings to pass through the mouth.

Materials   Workpiece from the last demonstration.

Tools   Carpenters' brace; 25mm auger bit; 6mm chisel; 12mm chisel; hammer or mallet, half-round file or sandpaper.

ACTIONS

1. Take a brace and 25mm bit and centre it on the mark 80mm from the front, 25mm from the sole. Bore out the throat to a depth of 20mm.

2. Make a freehand pencil line about 6mm from the edge of the hole, with a slight upward curve where it meets the frog.

3. Take a 6mm chisel and a hammer or mallet and chisel down at a slight angle from the 6mm line to the edge of the hole at the bottom. Cut the throat to the same depth as the frog.

4. Clean the bottom of the throat by scraping with a 12mm chisel. Smooth the side of the throat with a half-round file or sandpaper.

POINTS FOR EMPHASIS

o The angle of the throat helps to eject the shavings.
o Be careful not to split the short grain at the top of the throat.

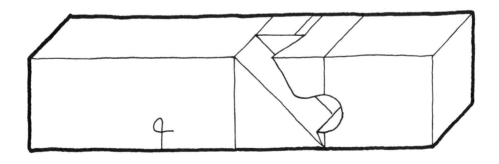

DEMO 4   Squaring up the mouth

Why   This allows the shavings to pass easily through the mouth.

Materials   Workpiece from the last demonstration.

Tools   Try-square; tenon-saw; 6mm chisel; 12mm chisel; pencil.

ACTIONS

1. Square a line on the bottom of the stock from the very front of the mouth.

2. Draw another line on the side of the stock, angled slightly towards the back.

3. Carefully saw the front of the mouth down to the gauge line.

4. Chisel out the waste with a small chisel and check again that the side of the throat is straight.

POINTS FOR EMPHASIS

o   Keep the mouth as small as possible.

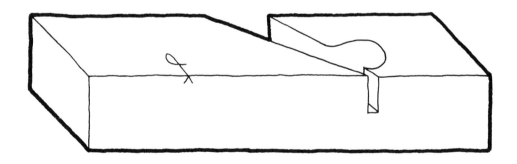

DEMO 5 Marking out and cutting the wedge

Why   The wedge holds the blade firmly in the stock of the plane.

Materials   One piece of hardwood 150 × 25 × 25mm.

Tools   Try-square; pencil; ripsaw; jack plane.

ACTIONS

1. Mark the main angle for the wedge, which should be about 100mm long.

2. Saw the angle of the wedge and plane the sawn edge.

3. Fit the wedge into the frog and check that there are no gaps on the face side. Ignore the gap in the middle.

4. The second angle of the wedge now has to be fitted to the throat. Set a marking gauge to 5mm and gauge the side of the wedge. The stock of the gauge must be held against the front of the wedge.

5. Plane the angle and fit it once more into the stock. This time there should be no gaps at all.

POINTS FOR EMPHASIS

o The wedge must fit well if it is to hold the blade tightly.
o The second angle prevents the wedge falling out when it is loosened.

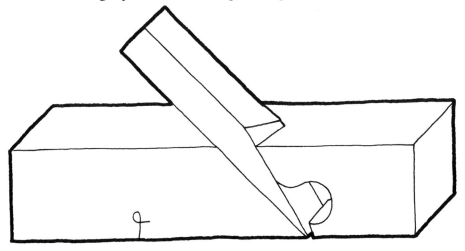

Rebate plane 69

DEMO 6   Fitting the wedge

Why   The wedge must allow the shavings to pass through the throat.

Materials   Workpiece from the last demonstration.

Tools   Pencil; tenon-saw; 25mm chisel; jack plane.

ACTIONS

1. Fit the blade you are going to use and wedge it in securely. (If the blade is tapered you may need to plane the wedge again).

2. Mark with a pencil a point 5mm below the top of the throat and draw in the double angle at the bottom of the wedge.

3. Mark a radius on the top of the wedge about 30mm from the top of the stock.

4. Saw off the small end of the wedge at the angle marked.

5. Saw off the top of the wedge and use a chisel to pare a slight radius.

6. Refit the blade and the wedge and check that the gap between the cutting edge and the front of the mouth is about 2mm.

7. Check that the side of the blade is slightly proud of the side of the stock. If necessary, plane the face side of the stock so that the blade allows about 0.5mm of clearance between the blade and the side of the plane.

POINTS FOR EMPHASIS

○ The second angle at the bottom of the wedge helps to push the shavings out of the throat of the plane.
○ Making the blade slightly proud of the stock allows the plane clearance from the rebate it is cutting, similar to the set of a handsaw.

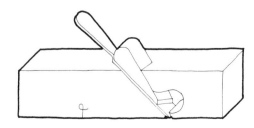

DEMO 7   Cutting the adjustment slots in fence

Why   The adjustment slots allow the fence to be moved to produce a rebate of any width up to 25mm.

Materials   One piece of hardwood 250 × 50 × 10mm.

Tools   Try-square; marking gauge; tape measure; pencil; 25mm chisel; 6mm chisel; mallet or hammer.

ACTIONS

1. Square lines all round, 30mm and 38mm from each end, to mark the sides of the adjustment slots.

2. Gauge a line 10mm from each edge on the top and bottom to mark the ends of the slots.

3. Mark the waste.

4. Use a 25mm chisel and a mallet or hammer to cut out the bulk of the waste. Cut halfway through from one side leaving about 1mm of waste before the line. Turn the work over and cut right through.

5. Finish paring the slot to the pencil lines.

6. Use a 6mm chisel to square the ends up to the gauge line.

POINTS FOR EMPHASIS

o   Cut the bulk of the waste out before cleaning up the ends.

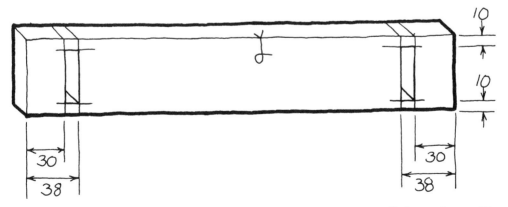

Rebate plane   71

DEMO 8　Drilling the holes for the adjustment screws

Why　　　　　The holes take the nuts and bolts which hold the fence firmly in position.

Materials　　The stock and fence; two 25 × 6mm nuts, bolts and washers.

Tools　　　　Try-square; marking gauge; pencil; tape measure; carpenters' brace; 12mm auger bit; wheel brace; 6mm twist bit.

ACTIONS

1. Place the fence in position on the sole of the plane (both ends should be flush). Mark the centre of the slots on the bottom of the plane.

2. Square lines across the sole and the side of the stock.

3. Set a marking gauge to 15mm and gauge the back of the stock, from the sole, to mark the holes for the nuts.

4. Measure a point 12mm from the back edge of the sole. Set a marking gauge to this point from the face side. Gauge the sole to mark the position of the holes for the adjustment screws.

5. Drill two 12mm holes in the side of the plane to a depth of 20mm.

6. Drill two 6mm holes in the sole of the plane to meet the first holes.

7. Place the fence in position; pass the bolts through the holes in the sole and the nuts through the holes in the side of the plane. Check that they align.

POINTS FOR EMPHASIS

o　Ask someone to check that the drill is square.

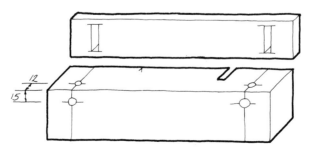

72　*Rebate plane*

DEMO 9 Chamfering the stock and the fence

Why   So that the plane is comfortable to hold.

Materials   Stock.

Tools   Jack plane; 25mm chisel; pencil; a coin.

ACTIONS

1. Mark radiuses by drawing round a coin on the sides of the stock, at the top of both ends.

2. Pare the corners back to the radius with a 25mm chisel and finish by planing them smooth in a vice.

3. Thumb-gauge lines 4mm from each edge on the front, top and back. Do not mark the sole.

4. Plane the straight chamfers down to the pencil lines and work the curved chamfers with a chisel.

5. Mark a radius on two corners of the fence using a pencil and a coin.

6. Plane and chisel the chamfers as before.

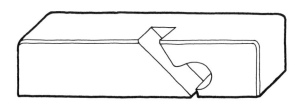

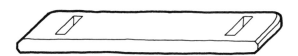

DEMO 10 Setting and using the rebate plane

Why

So that you can cut rebates in timber in order to let panels into frames and recesses, and to make picture frames and window casements.

Materials

One piece of scrap timber planed on the face side and face edge.

Tools

Completed rebate plane and blade; mallet.

ACTIONS

1. If necessary use a hacksaw to cut slots in the heads of the bolts, so that they can be tightened with a screwdriver.

2. Assemble the plane. Remember to place the washers between the fence and the head of the bolt.

3. Place the blade and wedge into the plane; tighten the wedge by hitting it gently with a mallet.

4. Set the fence for the required rebate, and make the screws thumb-tight. Check the setting at the front and the back of the plane and make any small adjustments necessary. Tighten the adjustment screws securely and recheck the setting.

5. To test the blade setting, clamp a piece of timber in a vice. Press the stock down onto the edge of the workpiece with the fence against the face of the workpiece, and try to take a shaving.

6. If the plane is cutting too deep, hit the back of the plane to bring back the blade and tap the wedge gently to tighten it again.

7. If the plane is not cutting, hit the top of the blade gently and tap the wedge to tighten it again. Repeat these actions until the plane cuts a fine, even shaving.

8. Start cutting about 100mm from the far end of the workpiece. Take longer and longer cuts until the rebate runs the full length, then work it down to the desired depth.

9. To remove the blade, simply hit the back of the stock until the wedge becomes loose.

SMOOTHING PLANE

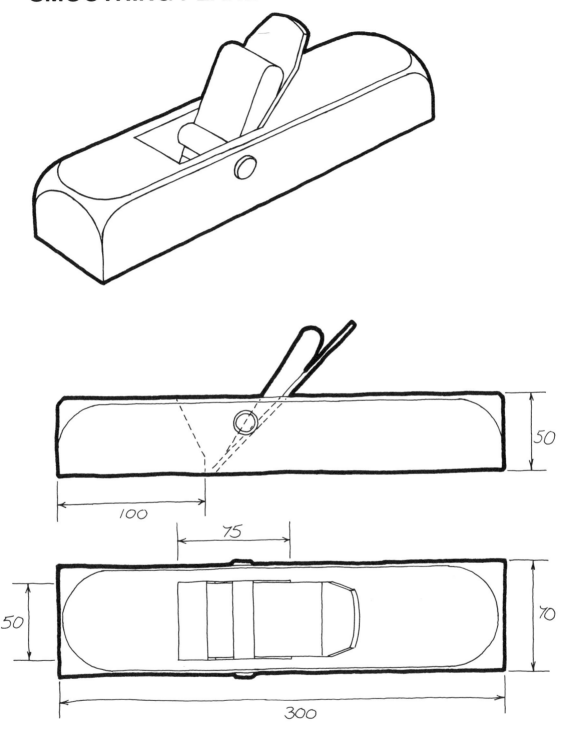

Objective

At the end of this session each participant will have made a smoothing plane.

Previous knowledge assumed

Competence in: preparing timber, marking out and cutting mortise and tenon joints.

Tools required

Try-square
Pencil
Steel rule or tape measure
Jack plane
Marking gauge
6mm chisel
12mm chisel

25mm chisel
Mallet
Carpenters' brace
18mm auger bit
Tenon-saw
Rasp

Common problems

Cutting the frog flat
Making the cheeks too thin
Cutting the mouth too big
Drilling the holes for the crossbar out of square

Cutting list

The instructor and each student need to prepare hardwood timber to the following dimensions (mm):

ITEM	QUANTITY	MATERIAL	L	W	T
Stock	1	Hardwood	300	70	50
Wedge	1	Hardwood	200	45	20
Crossbar	1	Hardwood	75	18	18

Also needed

45mm wide plane blade

Introduction

Time   One day.

What   In this session we are going to make a simple wooden smoothing plane.

Why   A smoothing plane is a valuable tool although not as essential as the larger jack plane. It is generally used for fine planing and smoothing up jointed work. Due to the shortage of foreign exchange in developing countries, imported steel planes are becoming so expensive that most graduate carpenters cannot afford to buy one, and practising carpenters are unable to replace their old ones.

    It is quicker and easier to make a plane from one piece of timber but it is often difficult to obtain timber of the right dimensions. This plane can be made from a 75 × 50mm stock which is easily available.

How   The session will be made up of a series of demonstrations. Each step will be demonstrated two or three times. I will ask some questions to check that the demonstration was clear, then you will practise the same operation. We will wait until everyone is finished before the next step is demonstrated.

This is the smoothing plane we are going to make. [SHOW TOOL TO TRAINEES] It works like this.

These are the parts.

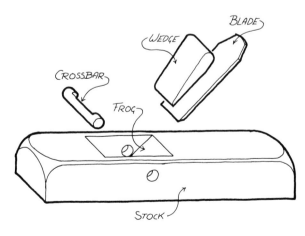

DEMO 1   Marking out the mouth and throat

Why   So that the frog and the throat can be cut out accurately.

Materials   One piece of hardwood 350 × 70 × 50mm.

Tools   Try-square; tape measure; marking gauge; pencil.

ACTIONS

1. Mark the front and the sole of the plane. The grain should rise towards the front.

2. Square two lines all round, 110mm and 106mm from the front, to mark the position of the mouth.

3. Check the thickness of the stock (this should be 50mm) and measure the same distance behind the second line on the top of the stock. This marks the back of the throat. Mark 45-degree diagonals on the sides of the stock.

4. Mark the front of the throat by measuring 20mm from the first line towards the front of the plane.

5. Set a marking gauge to 10mm and mark the sides of the throat on the top and bottom of the stock.

POINTS FOR EMPHASIS

o   Marking out should be done from the sole and both sides of the stock.
o   There will be less friction if the grain rises towards the front of the plane.

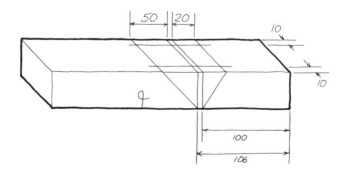

78   *Smoothing plane*

DEMO 2   Cutting out the mouth

Why   This makes it easier to chop out the frog and the throat in the next stage.

Materials   Workpiece from the last demonstration.

Tools   25mm chisel; 6mm chisel; mallet.

ACTIONS

1. Use a 25mm chisel and a mallet or hammer to cut out the bulk of the material, leaving about 1mm of waste before the lines.

2. Cut down to a depth of 10–15mm and finish paring the slot to the pencil lines.

3. Use a 6mm chisel to clean up the ends.

POINTS FOR EMPHASIS

o To cut the slot for the mouth cleanly, chisel out the bulk of the waste to within 2mm of the marked lines and when the mouth is at the right depth, finish paring up to the lines.

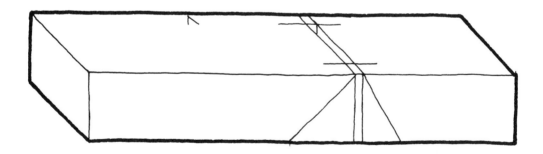

DEMO 3   Removing the waste from the throat

Why　　　　　A large amount of waste has to be removed before the frog
and the throat can be finished.

Materials　　Workpiece from the last demonstration.

Tools　　　　25mm chisel; mallet.

ACTIONS

1. Begin cutting out the throat by placing a 25mm chisel in the middle of the
    two lines marked for the mouth. The bevel of the chisel should face the
    back of the plane. Drive the chisel straight down with a mallet or hammer
    and then meet that cut by chiselling out a wedge of waste from behind the
    first cut.

2. Continue driving the chisel straight down between the lines. Follow each
    vertical cut with a diagonal cut that meets the first at 45°, directly over the
    mouth.

3. Finish cutting when you are within 5mm of the back of the throat and have
    reached the slot cut for the mouth.

POINTS FOR EMPHASIS

o Do not remove any waste from the front of the mouth.
o Each cut must be straight and meet the last cut directly over the mouth.
   Using this method the angle of the frog will be correct.

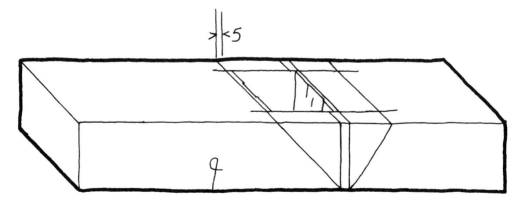

DEMO 4   Finishing the throat

Why   So that the blade of the plane will lie flat on the frog.

Materials   Workpiece from the last demonstration.

Tools   25mm chisel; 6mm chisel; mallet; plane blade.

ACTIONS

1. Chisel out the front of the throat at an angle to meet the mouth, about 10mm above the sole.

2. Pare the sides of the throat down to the gauge lines, making sure that the cheeks do not become too thin. Use a smaller chisel to reach down close to the mouth.

3. Carefully pare down the frog until it is flat and straight.

4. Use a plane blade to check that the frog is not twisted.

5. Check that the mouth of the plane is even.

POINTS FOR EMPHASIS

o The frog must be straight and flat, otherwise the blade will chatter and leave a rough finish.

o Check the frog with a straight edge regularly as you pare away the waste.

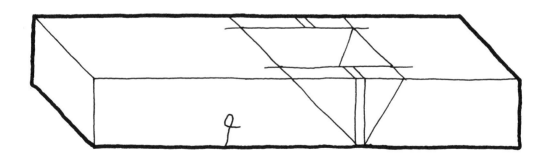

DEMO 5   Drilling the holes for the crossbar

Why   The crossbar passes through holes in the side of the plane.

Materials   Workpiece from the last demonstration; one piece of scrap timber roughly 50 × 50 × 100mm.

Tools   Try-square; tape measure; marking gauge; pencil; carpenters' brace; 18mm auger bit.

ACTIONS

1. Square a line on the sole of the plane 20mm behind the back of the mouth; continue the line round both sides of the plane.

2. Gauge a line on both sides of the stock, 32mm from the sole of the plane. This marks the centre of the holes for the crossbar.

3. To prevent the drill bit from splintering the inside of the throat, a piece of scrap timber, roughly 50 × 50mm, should be planed to fit tightly into the throat.

4. Place this piece of wood into the throat. Centre an 18mm drill bit where the gauge line crosses the pencil line, and drill right through the cheek. Ask for assistance to make sure the drill is square.

5. The hole on the other side of the stock is drilled in the same way.

POINTS FOR EMPHASIS

o All marking out must be done from the sole of the plane.
o These holes must be marked out and drilled accurately.

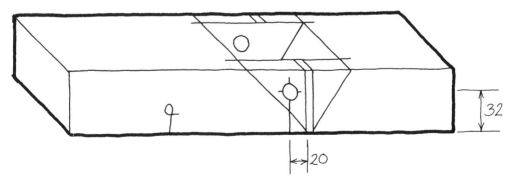

DEMO 6   Making the crossbar

Why   The crossbar acts against the wedge to hold the blade firmly
                 in position.

Materials   One piece of hardwood 75 × 18 × 18mm.

Tools   Try-square; marking gauge; pencil; tenon-saw; 25mm chisel.

ACTIONS

1. Square lines all round the stock, 15mm from each end, to mark the ends of
    the housing. Gauge a centre line on two opposite sides to mark the depth
    of the housing.

2. Plane the crossbar to an octagonal section.

3. Fit the crossbar into the holes in the side of the stock.

4. Make a series of saw cuts down to the gauge line, and chop out the waste
    with a chisel, first by driving the chisel along the grain from both ends and
    then by paring down across the grain.

POINTS FOR EMPHASIS

○ Do not saw below the gauge line.
○ Take care to keep fingers behind the cutting edge of the chisel.

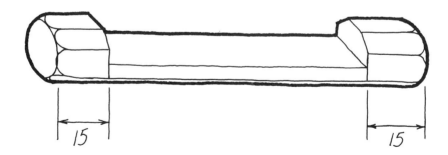

DEMO 7   Making the wedge

Why   The wedge holds the plane blade tightly against the frog of the plane.

Materials   One piece of hardwood 200 × 45 × 20mm.

Tools   Try-square; ruler; pencil; ripsaw; jack plane; 25mm chisel.

ACTIONS

1.   Square a line all round 100mm from one end, and mark the angle for the wedge. Square another line 130mm from the same end to mark the top of the wedge.

2.   Use a ripsaw to cut the angle of the wedge, and plane the sawn face square and smooth.

3.   Saw off the end of the wedge with a tenon-saw, and round off the top by paring the end grain with a chisel.

4.   Chamfer the thin end of the wedge to allow the shavings to pass over it easily.

POINTS FOR EMPHASIS

○   Rounding off the top of the wedge will prevent it splitting when struck with a hammer.

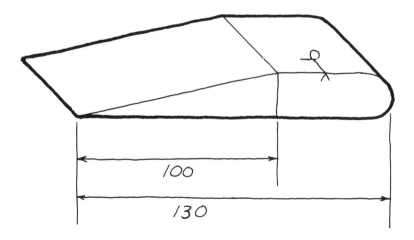

DEMO 8   Shaping the stock

Why   So that the plane is comfortable to use.

Materials   Workpiece from the last demonstration; stock.

Tools   Jack plane; 25mm chisel; pencil; small tin.

ACTIONS

1. Thumb-gauge a line all round the top of the stock, 4mm from each edge, to mark the chamfers.

2. Mark radiuses on the top, sides, front, and back and the back of the stock. Drawing round a small tin will help to make the radiuses even.

3. Plane the chamfers down to the pencil lines on both sides, and use a wide chisel to round off the corners.

4. Fit the wedge into the stock (there should be 1–2mm clearance at the side); sandpaper the stock and the wedge smooth.

POINTS FOR EMPHASIS

○ The appearance of the plane will be improved if the chamfers are even.
○ The clearance between the wedge and the throat allows the wedge to be removed easily.

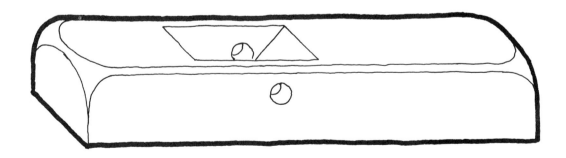

DEMO 9   Fitting the blade

Why   So that the plane will leave a straight, smooth surface without becoming choked.

Materials   Plane stock; blade; wedge; crossbar.

Tools   25mm chisel; mallet or hammer; straight edge; jack plane.

ACTIONS

1. If you have bought a blade from a hardware shop it may be too wide to fit. The sides will have to be ground to give a clearance of about 3mm.

2. If the blade you are going to use has been made by a blacksmith it may be too thick to fit through the mouth. Square a line on the sole, 1mm from the front of the mouth, and open it out with a hammer and chisel. Repeat this process until there is a gap of about 3–4mm between the front of the blade and the front of the mouth.

3. Position the blade so that the cutting edge is about 5mm inside the throat, and wedge it tight. Clamp the plane upside down in a vice and plane the sole straight and true.

POINTS FOR EMPHASIS

○ When grinding a plane blade take care not to get it too hot as it will lose its temper and become soft.
○ Clearance between the blade and the side of the throat allows some lateral adjustment.
○ If the mouth is made too big it will leave a rough finish on crossgrain timber. If it is too small the plane will become choked when used.
○ The wedge tends to bend the stock of the plane when it is tight, so the sole should be trued up when the blade and wedge are in position.

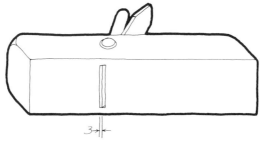

86   *Smoothing plane*

DEMO 10   Setting and using the plane

Why   So that you can become accustomed to adjusting and using
                 the plane.

Materials   One piece of scrap timber.

Tools   Finished jack plane; small hammer.

ACTIONS

1. Hold the stock of the plane with one finger underneath the mouth. Put the
   blade into the throat and let it rest on your finger so that it does not project
   below the sole of the plane.

2. Place the wedge between the blade and the crossbar.

3. Tap the wedge gently with a hammer to tighten it.

4. Test the setting.

5. If the plane is not cutting, hit the top of the blade gently, and tap the
   wedge to tighten it again.

6. If the plane is cutting too deep, hit the back of the plane to bring back the
   blade and tap the wedge gently to tighten it again.

7. Look along the bottom of the plane to make sure the cutting edge is
   parallel to the sole. If one corner is too high, tap the opposite side of the
   blade.

8. Repeat these actions until the plane cuts a fine, even shaving.

9. To remove the blade, simply hit the back of the stock until the wedge
   becomes loose.

ONE-PIECE JACK PLANE

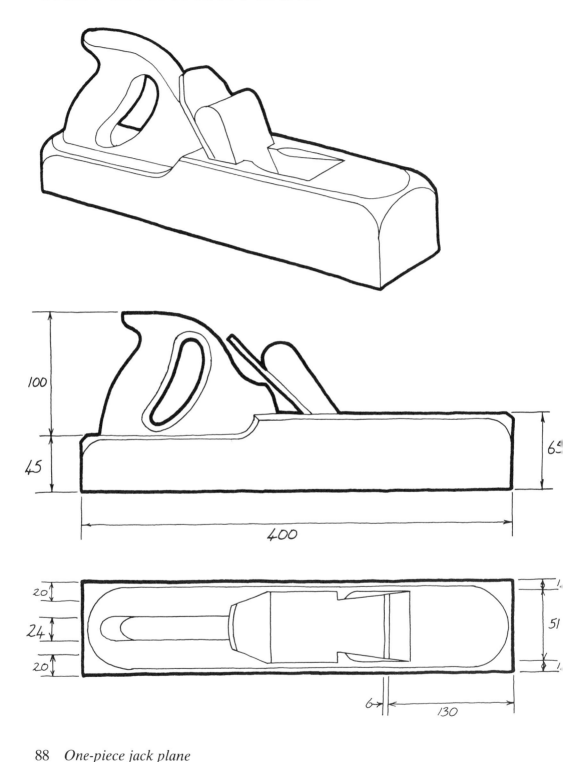

Objective

At the end of this session each participant will have made a jack plane.

Previous knowledge assumed

Competence in: preparing timber, marking out and cutting mortise and tenon joints.

Tools required

Try-square
Straight edge
Pencil
Steel rule or tape measure
Jack plane
Marking gauge
6mm chisel
12mm chisel

25mm chisel
Mallet
Tenon-saw
Ripsaw
Bow-saw
Hacksaw
Half-round file
Spokeshave

Common problems

Cutting the frog at the wrong angle
Cutting the mouth too big
Cutting the wedge grip out of alignment
Fitting the handle too close to the blade

Cutting list

The instructor and each student need to prepare hardwood timber to the following dimensions (mm):

ITEM	QUANTITY	MATERIAL	L	W	T
Stock	1	Hardwood	400	75	65
Wedge	1	Hardwood	200	50	20
Handle	1	Hardwood	130	110	25

Also needed

50mm wide plane blade

Introduction

Time   Two days.

What   In this session we are all going to make a wooden jack plane.

Why   Every carpenter needs a jack plane for smoothing and plan-
                ing timber to the required width and thickness. Due to the
                shortage of foreign currency, imported steel planes are be-
                coming so expensive that most graduate carpenters in de-
                veloping countries cannot afford to buy one, and practising
                carpenters cannot afford to replace their old ones.
                    This method of construction requires quite a heavy section
                of timber to make the stock. If such a section is unavailable it
                will be necessary to glue together two pieces to make the
                right section, or to follow the instructions in the next section.

How   The session will be made up of a series of demonstrations.
                Each step will be demonstrated two or three times. I will ask
                some questions to check that the demonstration was clear,
                then you will practise the same operation. We will wait until
                everyone is finished before the next step is demonstrated.

This is the jack plane we are going to make. [SHOW TOOL TO TRAINEES]
It works like this.

These are the parts.

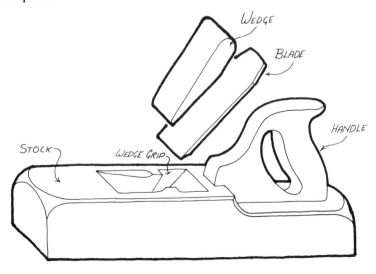

90   *One-piece jack plane*

DEMO 1   Marking out the mouth and throat

Why   So that the throat can be cut out accurately.

Materials   One piece of hardwood 400 × 75 × 65mm.

Tools   Try-square; tape measure; marking gauge; pencil.

ACTIONS

1. Mark the front and the sole of the plane. The grain should rise towards the front.

2. Mark the angle for the frog and the front of the throat as shown in the drawing.

3. On the top, mark the front of the throat by measuring 20mm from the first line towards the front of the plane.

4. Set a marking gauge to 12mm and mark the outer sides of the throat on the top and bottom of the stock.

5. Set a marking gauge to 20mm and mark the inner sides of the throat on the top and bottom of the stock.

6. Mark the waste between the two inner lines.

POINTS FOR EMPHASIS

o   Marking out should be done from the sole and both sides of the stock.
o   There will be less friction if the grain rises towards the front.

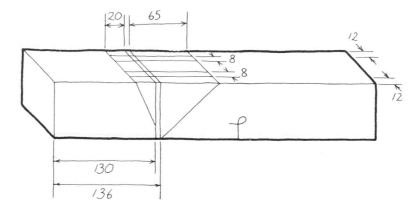

One-piece jack plane   91

DEMO 2 Cutting out the mouth

Why This makes it easier to chop out the frog and the throat in the next stage.

Materials Workpiece from the last demonstration.

Tools 25mm chisel; 6mm chisel; mallet.

ACTIONS

1. To make it easier to chisel the correct angle for the frog, a slot for the mouth should be cut into the sole of the plane. Remove the waste between the two inner gauge lines.

2. Use a 25mm chisel and a mallet or hammer to cut the bulk of the waste out, leaving about 1mm before the lines. Cut down to a depth of 10–15mm.

3. Pare the slot back to the pencil and gauge lines.

4. Use a 6mm chisel to clean up the ends of the slot.

POINTS FOR EMPHASIS

o Remove the waste between the two inner gauge lines only.
o To cut a clean mouth, remove the bulk of the waste before cleaning up the edges.

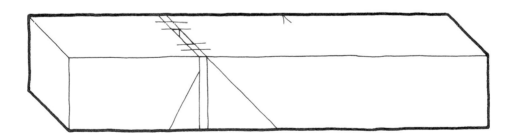

DEMO 3   Removing the waste from the throat

Why   A large amount of waste has to be removed before the frog
                      and the throat can be finished.

Materials   Workpiece from the last demonstration.

Tools   25mm chisel; mallet.

ACTIONS

1. Begin cutting out the throat by placing a 25mm chisel in the middle of the
    two lines marked for the mouth. The bevel of the chisel should face the
    back of the plane. Drive the chisel straight down with a mallet or hammer
    and then meet that cut by chiselling out a wedge of waste from behind the
    first cut.

2. Continue driving the chisel straight down over the mouth, meeting each
    cut by chiselling out the waste at an angle from behind the first cut.

3. Finish cutting when you are within 5mm of the back of the throat and have
    reached the slot cut for the mouth.

POINTS FOR EMPHASIS

o   Remove waste from between the two inner gauge lines only.
o   Do not remove any waste from the front of the mouth.
o   Each cut must be straight and should meet the last cut directly over the
    mouth. Using this method, the angle of the frog will be correct.

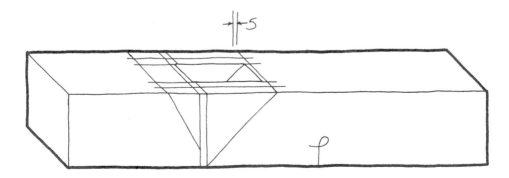

One-piece jack plane   93

DEMO 4   Finishing the throat

Why   So that the blade of the plane will lie flat on the frog.

Materials   Workpiece from the last demonstration.

Tools   25mm chisel; 6mm chisel; mallet or hammer; straight edge.

ACTIONS

1. Chisel out the front of the throat at an angle to meet the mouth about 10mm above the sole.

2. Pare the sides of the throat down to the gauge lines, making sure that the cheeks do not become too thin. Use a smaller chisel to reach down close to the mouth.

3. Carefully pare down the frog until it is flat and straight.

4. Use a straight edge to check that the frog is straight.

5. Check that the mouth of the plane is even.

POINTS FOR EMPHASIS

○ The frog must be straight and flat; otherwise the blade will chatter and leave a rough finish.

○ Check the frog with a straight edge regularly as you pare away the waste.

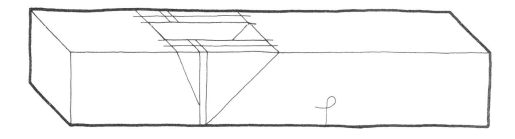

DEMO 5   Sawing the front of the throat and the wedge grip

Why   This makes it easier to remove the waste from the wedge grip and to shape the cheeks.

Materials   Workpiece from the last demonstration.

Tools   Ruler; try-square; pencil; hacksaw.

ACTIONS

1. Mark the front of the wedge grip as shown in the drawing.

2. Remove the blade from a hacksaw, thread it through the mouth of the plane and fix it back to the frame, making sure the teeth point forward.

3. Clamp the stock of the plane, on its side, securely to the bench. Hold the blade against the front of the throat and saw down the waste side of the pencil line. Stop when you reach the gauge lines.

4. Position the saw on the waste side of the line that marks the wedge grip on the top of the stock, and against the front of the mouth on the sole of the stock. Saw down to the gauge line.

5. Hold the blade against the frog and saw down to the gauge line.

6. Reposition the blade in the frame of the saw to cut the other side of the throat in the same way.

POINTS FOR EMPHASIS

o   Saw on the waste side of the lines.
o   Do not saw below the gauge lines.

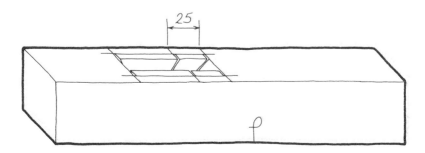

DEMO 6 Removing the waste from the cheeks and the wedge grips

Why So that the wedge can be fitted and to allow the shavings to pass easily through the throat.

Materials Workpiece from the last demonstration.

Tools 25mm chisel; 12mm chisel; 6mm chisel; mallet.

ACTIONS

1. Use a 6mm chisel to remove the waste from the wedge grip, as close to the mouth as possible.

2. Use a 25mm chisel to cut away the sides of the cheek at an angle that opens out to the front of the throat.

3. Flare out the bottom 15mm of the throat to the full width of the mouth. This helps the shavings to pass easily through the mouth.

4. Using a straight edge, check the sides of the wedge grip are straight.

5. A stopped chamfer can be cut on the top of the cheeks to form the 'eyes' of the plane.

POINTS FOR EMPHASIS

○ Take care to leave a large surface for the wedge to bear against.
○ Do not make the stock of the plane weak by cutting the cheeks too thin.
○ The stopped chamfers improve the appearance of the plane, and make the edge less likely to splinter.

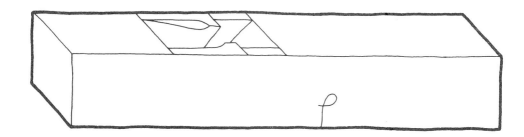

DEMO 7 Shaping the back of the stock

Why   To make the plane easier to handle.

Materials   Workpiece from the last demonstration.

Tools   Try-square; marking gauge; ruler; pencil; ripsaw; jack plane;
                 25mm chisel; cabinet scraper.

ACTIONS

1. Mark out the back of the stock as shown in the drawing, using a small tin
   to draw the radius.

2. Remove the bulk of the waste with a ripsaw, as close to the marks as
   possible.

3. Plane and scrape the sawn face down to the gauge line.

4. Use a 25mm chisel to cut and smooth the curve. The bevel of the chisel
   should face the front of the plane so it can be used to control the cut.

5. Scrape and sandpaper the back of the stock smooth.

POINTS FOR EMPHASIS

○ Saw on the waste side of the line.
○ By removing a section from the back of the stock and allowing the handle
   to be closer to the sole, you will find that the plane becomes much easier to
   control.

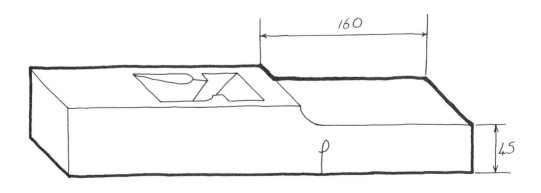

One-piece jack plane 97

DEMO 8   Marking out the handle

Why   So that the handle can be cut to shape.

Materials   One piece of hardwood 130 × 110 × 25mm.

Tools   Try-square; ruler; marking gauge; pencil.

ACTIONS

1. Mark out the housing joints at the front and back of the handle.

2. Mark the position of the holes. [See the drawing for dimensions.]

3. Drill a 25mm hole in the top of the handle and a 20mm hole in the bottom.

4. Mark out the shape of the handle as close as possible to the drawing.

POINTS FOR EMPHASIS

o   Drill halfway through from both sides, meeting in the middle.

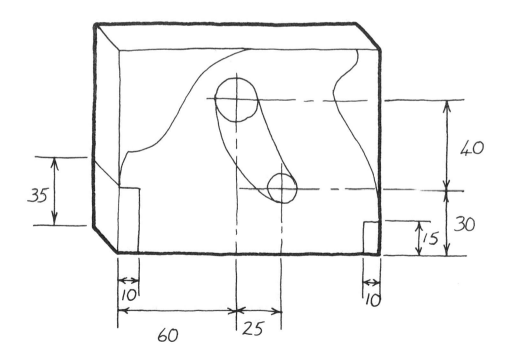

98   *One-piece jack plane*

Cutting out the handle

Why   So that the handle can be shaped.

Materials   Workpiece from the last demonstration.

Tools   Bow-saw; tenon-saw.

ACTIONS

1. Position the handle in the vice.

2. A bow-saw can be used to cut the inside of the handle. Thread the blade through one of the holes, tighten the frame and saw as normal.

3. Use a bow-saw to cut the outside shape of the handle.

4. Cut the housing joints in the front and back of the handle, using a tenon-saw.

POINTS FOR EMPHASIS

o   Remember to keep the blade of the saw square to the work.

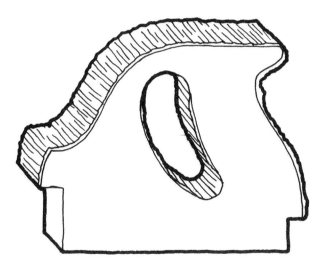

One-piece jack plane   99

DEMO 10   Shaping the handle

Why   So that the handle is comfortable to hold.

Materials   Workpiece from the last demonstration.

Tools   Pencil; half-round file; spokeshave; chisel; sandpaper.

ACTIONS

1.   Use a chisel or a spokeshave to clean up the top edge.

2.   Thumb-gauge lines 6mm from the edge on the back, the inside and the sides of the handle, but do not mark the top or the bottom.

3.   Chamfer the edges down to the pencil lines with a chisel, remembering always to cut with the grain.

4.   Finally, carve the handle smooth and round. The chamfers should help to make the curves even. A fine half-round file and some sandpaper will help to finish the job well.

POINTS FOR EMPHASIS

o   The appearance of the handle will be improved if the handle is shaped evenly.

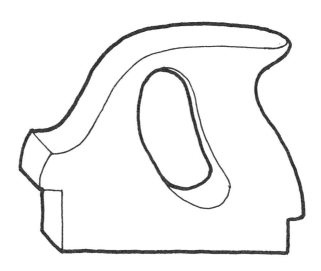

DEMO 11   Cutting the mortise for the handle

Why   So that the handle can be jointed to the stock.

Materials   Workpiece from the last demonstration; stock.

Tools   Try-square; marking gauge; pencil; ruler; 20mm chisel; 25mm chisel; mallet or hammer.

ACTIONS

1. Square a line across the back of the stock 110mm from the top of the curve.

2. Gauge two lines in the centre of the stock, 24mm apart. The mortise will run from the pencil line to the top of the curve.

3. Mark the waste.

4. Check the gauge lines by offering the handle up to the stock.

5. Chop out the mortise to a depth of 15mm at the back of the plane.

6. Carefully pare the sides of the mortise to the gauge lines.

7. Fit the handle into the stock but do not glue it in place yet.

POINTS FOR EMPHASIS

o   If the handle is glued in now it will be difficult to chamfer the stock in the next stage.

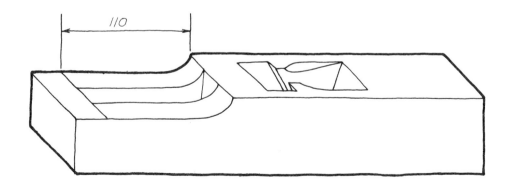

DEMO 12 Chamfering the stock

Why   To make the plane comfortable to hold.

Materials   Workpieces from the last demonstrations.

Tools   Jack plane; 25mm chisel; pencil; small tin.

ACTIONS

1. Thumb-gauge a line all round the top of the stock, 4mm from each edge, to mark the chamfers.

2. Mark radiuses on the top, sides, front and back of the stock. A small tin may help to make the curves even.

3. Plane the chamfers down to the pencil lines on both sides. You will have to use a chisel on the curve in the middle of the stock. Then use a wide chisel to round off the corners.

4. The handle can now be glued into position. Use a clamp to push it tightly into the mortise.

POINTS FOR EMPHASIS

o The appearance of the plane will be improved if the chamfers are even.

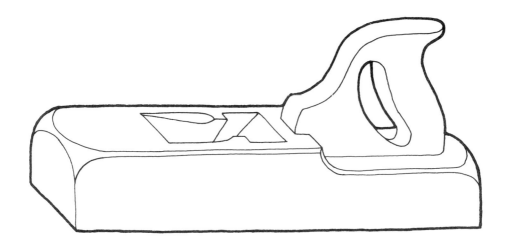

DEMO 13   Making the wedge

Why   The wedge holds the plane blade tightly against the frog of
               the plane.

Materials   One piece of hardwood 200 × 50 × 20mm.

Tools   Try-square; ruler; pencil; ripsaw; jack plane; 25mm chisel.

ACTIONS

1. Square a line all round 100mm from one end, and mark the angle for the
    wedge. Square another line 130mm from the same end to mark the top of
    the wedge.

2. Use a ripsaw to cut the angle of the wedge, and plane the sawn face square
    and smooth.

3. Saw off the end of the wedge with a tenon-saw; round off the top by paring
    the end grain with a chisel.

4. Chamfer the thin end of the wedge to allow the shavings to pass over it
    easily.

POINTS FOR EMPHASIS

o   Radiusing the top of the wedge will prevent it from splitting when struck
    with a hammer.

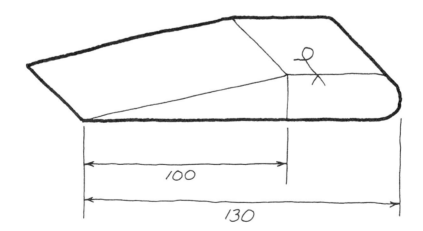

One-piece jack plane   103

DEMO 14 Fitting the blade

Why So that the plane will leave a straight, smooth surface without becoming choked.

Materials Plane stock; blade; wedge; crossbar.

Tools 25mm chisel; mallet or hammer; straight edge; jack plane.

ACTIONS

1. If you have bought a blade from a hardware shop it should fit easily into the throat and through the mouth.

2. If the blade you are going to use has been made by a blacksmith it may be too thick to fit through the mouth. Square a line on the sole, 1mm from the front of the mouth, and open it out with a hammer and chisel. Repeat this process until there is a gap of about 3–4mm between the front of the blade and the front of the mouth.

3. Position the blade so that that the cutting edge is about 5mm inside the throat and wedge it tight. Clamp the plane upside down in a vice and plane the sole straight and true.

POINTS FOR EMPHASIS

o Clearance between the blade and the side of the throat allows some lateral adjustment.
o If the mouth is made too big it will leave a rough finish on crossgrain timber. If it is too small the plane will become choked when used.
o The wedge tends to bend the stock of the plane when it is tight, so the sole should be trued up when the blade and wedge are in position.

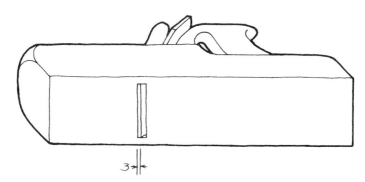

104 *One-piece jack plane*

DEMO 15   Setting and using the plane

Why   So you can become accustomed to adjusting and using the
               plane.

Materials   One piece of scrap timber.

Tools   Finished jack plane; small hammer.

ACTIONS

1. Hold the stock of the plane with one finger underneath the mouth. Put the blade into the throat and let it rest on your finger, so that it does not project below the sole of the plane.

2. Place the wedge into the wedge grips.

3. Tap the wedge gently with a hammer to tighten it.

4. Test the setting.

5. If the plane is not cutting, hit the top of the blade gently and tap the wedge to tighten it again.

6. If the plane is cutting too deep, hit the back of the plane to bring back the blade, and tap the wedge gently to tighten it again.

7. Look along the bottom of the plane to make sure the cutting edge is parallel to the sole. If one corner is too high, tap the opposite side of the blade.

8. Repeat these actions until the plane cuts a fine, even shaving.

9. To remove the blade, simply hit the back of the stock until the wedge becomes loose.

TWO-PIECE JACK PLANE

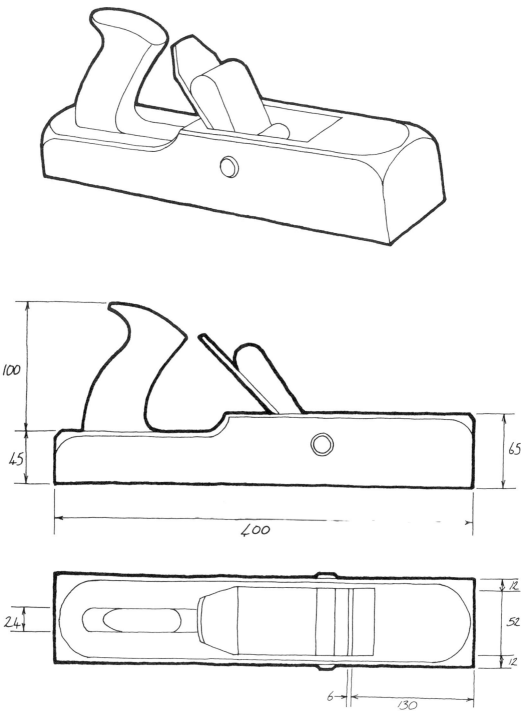

106   *Two-piece jack plane*

Objective

At the end of this session each participant will have made a jack plane.

Previous knowledge assumed

Competence in: preparing timber, marking out and cutting mortise and tenon joints.

Tools required

Try-square
Straight edge
Pencil
Steel rule or tape measure
Jack plane
Marking gauge
6mm chisel
12mm chisel
25mm chisel

Mallet
5 'G' clamps or sash clamps
Carpenters' brace
18mm auger bit
Tenon-saw
Ripsaw
Bow-saw
Half-round file
Spokeshave

Common problems

Cutting the two halves of the throat
Cutting the mouth too big
Cutting the holes for the crossbar out of square
Fitting the handle too close to the blade

Cutting list

The instructor and each student need to prepare hardwood timber to the following dimensions (mm):

ITEM	QUANTITY	MATERIAL	L	W	T
Stock	2	Hardwood	400	65	40
Crossbar	1	Hardwood	80	18	18
Wedge	1	Hardwood	200	50	20
Handle	1	Hardwood	100	115	25

Also needed

50mm wide plane blade; PVA wood glue

Introduction

Time   Two days.

What   In this session we are all going to make a wooden jack plane.

Why   Every carpenter needs a jack plane for smoothing and plan-
         ing timber to the required width and thickness. Due to the
         shortage of foreign currency, imported steel planes are be-
         coming so expensive that most graduate carpenters in de-
         veloping countries cannot afford to buy one, and practising
         carpenters cannot afford to replace their old ones.
             This method of construction can be used where it is diffi-
         cult to obtain timber of the right size to produce a plane
         from one piece.

How   The session will be made up of a series of demonstrations.
         Each step will be demonstrated two or three times. I will ask
         some questions to check that the demonstration was clear,
         then you will practise the same operation. We will wait until
         everyone is finished before the next step is demonstrated.

This is the jack plane we are going to make. [SHOW TOOL TO TRAINEES]
It works like this.

These are the parts.

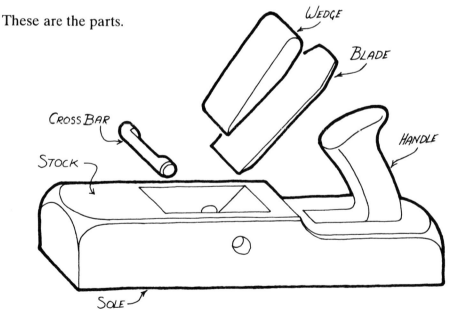

DEMO 1   Preparing the joint between the two halves of the stock

Why   For the glue to work well the two surfaces must be in contact throughout the joint.

Materials   Two pieces of hardwood 400 × 65 × 40mm.

Tools   Jack plane; pencil; straight edge.

ACTIONS

1. Choose the faces to form the joint between the two halves, and mark the front and the sole of the plane. The grain should rise towards the front.

2. Plane the two inside edges to form a well-fitting butt joint. There should be no visible gaps between the two pieces.

3. Mark the inside faces as the face sides and check that the face edges are square.

POINTS FOR EMPHASIS

o   Both faces should be straight and not in twist.
o   Wood glue will only work when the two pieces of the joint are in contact, so they must be well planed.

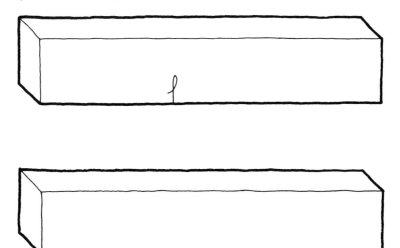

Two-piece jack plane   109

DEMO 2   Marking out the stock

Why   So that the throat can be cut out accurately. The stock of the
               plane will be formed when the two pieces are fixed together.

Materials   Workpieces from the last demonstration.

Tools   Try-square; marking gauge; ruler; pencil.

ACTIONS

1.   Gauge both pieces to a thickness of 38mm.

2.   Hold the two parts of the stock together and mark the position of the
     mouth on the sole of the plane, 130mm from the front.

3.   Mark out the front of the throat and the frog, as shown in the drawings.

4.   Set a marking gauge to 26mm and gauge the width of the throat on both
     pieces, top and bottom.

5.   Mark the waste.

6.   Check that the two pieces are marked out equally.

POINTS FOR EMPHASIS

o   The waste will be planed from the sides of the stock after it has been glued
     together.
o   All marking out must be done from the face side or the face edge.
o   Note that the two pieces are mirror images of each other.

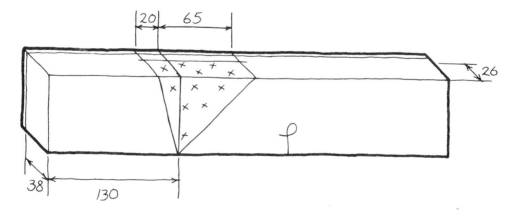

110   *Two-piece jack plane*

DEMO 3   Cutting the throat

Why   To form the frog, throat and mouth from both pieces of timber.

Materials   Workpieces from the last demonstration.

Tools   Tenon-saw; 25mm chisel; 6mm chisel.

ACTIONS

1. Use a tenon-saw to cut down the waste side of the lines at the frog and the **front** of the throat.

2. **Make** three or four cuts in the throat to make it easier to chisel out the **waste**. Take care not to cut below the gauge line.

3. Use a 25mm chisel to remove the bulk of the waste.

4. **Square** a line across the front of the throat, 6mm from the back of the **mouth**.

5. Use a tenon-saw to open up the mouth.

6. **Chisel** out the remainder of the throat with a 6mm chisel and check that **the ch**eek is straight.

7. **Repe**at this process on the other half of the stock.

POINTS FOR EMPHASIS

o   **Saw on** the waste side of the lines.
o   **Do not** saw below the gauge lines as this will weaken the stock.

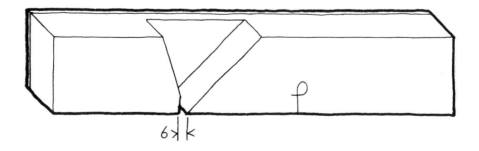

DEMO 4   Gluing the stock together

Why   To form the stock of the plane.

Materials   Workpieces from the last demonstration; a piece of scrap
               timber 400mm long.

Tools   Five 'G' clamps/sash clamps; wood glue; damp cloth; con-
               tainer of water.

ACTIONS

1. Clamp the two pieces of the stock together and make sure the joint still fits
    well. Do not apply glue. Use at least one clamp at the front and two clamps
    at the back.

2. Unclamp the stock and spread a thin layer of glue over both pieces. (If the
    timber is very dense, first lightly sandpaper the surfaces to be glued across
    the grain.)

3. Place the two parts of the stock together, with a small piece of scrap timber
    below the join. Line up the two halves of the throat and position a clamp at
    each end so that the shoes are above and below the join. This prevents the
    two pieces from sliding across each other.

4. Next, place one clamp across the front and another across the back, and
    tighten until some of the glue is squeezed out of the joint.

5. Remove the first clamps and place them on the back of the plane. Check
    that the throat is still aligned.

6. Wipe off the excess glue with a wet rag, and allow it to set for six hours.

POINTS FOR EMPHASIS

o   Sandpapering the surfaces to be glued tears the fibres and will help the
    wood absorb glue.
o   Do not clamp the joint too tightly as this may squeeze out too much glue.

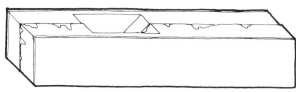

112   *Two-piece jack plane*

Planing the stock and truing up the throat

Why   So that the blade lies flat on the frog, and is square to the sole.

Materials   Workpiece from the last demonstration.

Tools   Jack plane; try-square; pencil; 25mm chisel.

ACTIONS

1. Plane the sides of the stock down to the gauge lines.

2. Mark one side as the face side.

3. Plane the top and bottom of the stock square to the new face side.

4. Use a 25mm chisel to true up the front and back of the throat.

5. Check that the frog is flat, using a plane blade or a straight edge.

POINTS FOR EMPHASIS

o The frog of the plane must be flat; otherwise the blade will chatter and leave a rough finish.

o All marking out must be done from the new face side and face edge.

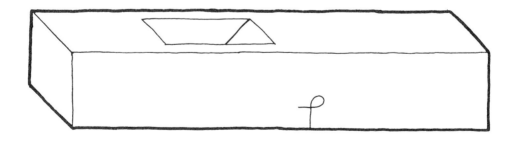

Two-piece jack plane   113

DEMO 6   Drilling the holes for the crossbar

Why   The crossbar passes through holes in the side of the plane.

Materials   Workpiece from the last demonstration; one piece of scrap timber, roughly 55 × 50 × 100mm.

Tools   Try-square; tape measure; marking gauge; pencil; carpenters' brace; 18mm drill bit.

ACTIONS

1. Square a line on the sole of the plane, 15mm behind the back of the mouth, and continue these lines round both sides of the plane.

2. Gauge a line across the pencil lines on both sides of the stock, 40mm from the sole of the plane. This marks the centre of the holes for the crossbar.

3. To prevent the drill bit from splintering the inside of the throat, a piece of scrap timber, roughly 55 × 50mm, should be planed to fit tightly into the throat.

4. Centre an 18mm drill bit on the two lines just marked and drill right through the cheek. Ask for assistance to make sure the drill is square.

5. The hole on the other side of the stock is drilled in the same way.

POINTS FOR EMPHASIS

○ All marking out must be done from the sole of the plane and the face side.
○ The crossbar holes must be marked out and drilled accurately.

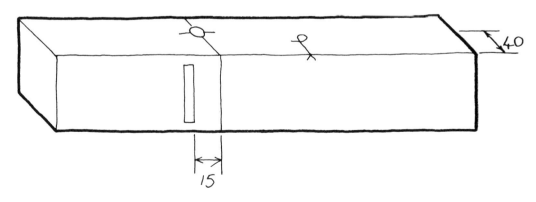

114   *Two-piece jack plane*

DEMO 7   Making the crossbar

Why   The crossbar acts against the wedge to hold the blade firmly in position.

Materials   One piece of hardwood $80 \times 18 \times 18$mm.

Tools   Try-square; marking gauge; pencil; tenon-saw; 25mm chisel.

ACTIONS

1. Square lines all round, 15mm from each end, to mark the ends of the housing. Gauge a centre line on two opposite sides to mark the depth of the housing.

2. Plane the crossbar to an octagonal section.

3. Fit the crossbar into the holes in the side of the stock.

4. Make a series of saw cuts down to the gauge line. Chop out the waste with a chisel, first by driving the chisel along the grain from both ends and then by paring down across the grain.

POINTS FOR EMPHASIS

o Do not saw below the gauge line.
o Take care to keep fingers behind the cutting edge of the chisel.

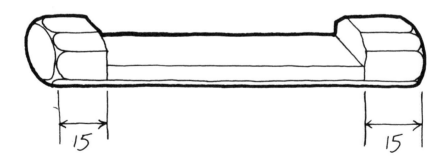

DEMO 8   Shaping the back of the stock

Why   To make the plane easier to handle.

Materials   The assembled plane stock.

Tools   Try-square; marking gauge; ruler; pencil; ripsaw; jack plane; 25mm chisel; cabinet scraper.

ACTIONS

1. Square a line across the top of the stock 160mm from the back, and continue this line down both sides.

2. Set a marking gauge to 45mm and gauge all round the back of the stock up to the pencil lines.

3. Use a small tin to mark a radius from the pencil line down to the gauge line, on both sides.

4. Remove the bulk of the waste with a ripsaw, as close to the marks as possible.

5. Plane and scrape the sawn face down to the gauge line.

6. Use a 25mm chisel to cut and smooth the curve. The bevel of the chisel should face the front of the plane so it can be used to control the cut.

7. Scrape and sandpaper the back of the stock smooth.

POINTS FOR EMPHASIS

o   Saw on the waste side of the line.
o   By removing a section from the back of the stock and allowing the handle to be closer to the sole, you will find that the plane becomes easier to control.

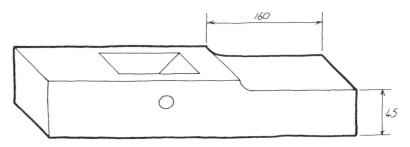

116   *Two-piece jack plane*

Marking out the handle

Why   So that the handle can be cut to shape.

Materials   One piece of hardwood 100 × 115 × 25mm.

Tools   Try-square; ruler; marking gauge; pencil.

ACTIONS

1. Gauge a line all round, 20mm from the bottom. Mark a 10mm-long shoulder in the back of the handle, and mark the position of the two holes as shown in the drawing.

2. Use a brace and a 20mm bit to drill out the two holes.

3. The shape of the handle can now be drawn in.

POINTS FOR EMPHASIS

o   Drilling these holes will help to mark out the handle and makes it easier to cut the tight curves.

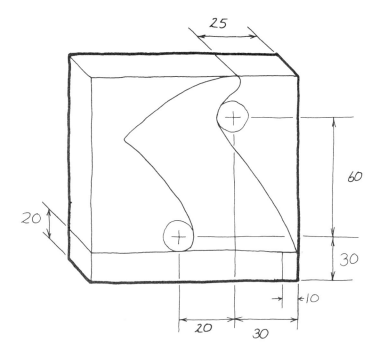

Two-piece jack plane   117

DEMO 10 Cutting out the handle

Why   So that the handle can be shaped.

Materials   Workpiece from the last demonstration.

Tools   Bow-saw; tenon-saw.

ACTIONS

1. Position the handle in the vice.

2. Cut out the shape of the bow-saw, remembering to keep the blade **square** to the workpiece.

3. Cut the housing joint in the back of the handle, using a tenon-saw.

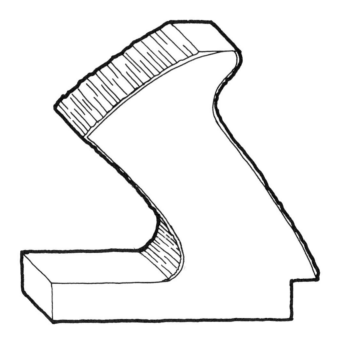

DEMO 11 Shaping the handle

Why   So that the handle is comfortable to hold.

Materials   Workpiece from the last demonstration.

Tools   Pencil; half-round file; chisel; sandpaper; spokeshave.

ACTIONS

1. Use a chisel or a spokeshave to clean up the top edge.

2. Thumb-gauge lines 6mm from the edge on the back and front of the handle, but do not mark the two top edges or the bottom.

3. Chamfer the edges down to the pencil lines with a chisel, remembering always to cut with the grain.

4. Finally, carve the handle smooth and round. The chamfers should help to make the curves even. A half-round file and some sandpaper will help to finish the job well.

POINTS FOR EMPHASIS

○ The appearance of the handle will be improved if the handle is shaped evenly.

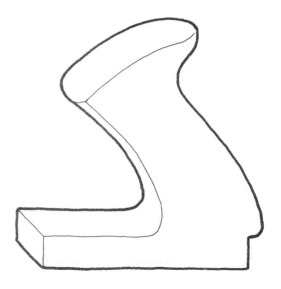

Two-piece jack plane 119

DEMO 12   Cutting the mortise for the handle

Why   So that the handle can be jointed to the stock.

Materials   Workpiece from the last demonstration; stock.

Tools   Try-square; marking gauge; pencil; ruler; 20mm chisel; 25mm chisel; mallet or hammer.

ACTIONS

1. Square two lines across the back of the stock, 50mm and 140mm from the back of the plane.

2. Gauge two lines, 24mm apart, in the centre of the stock.

3. Mark the waste.

4. Check the gauge lines by offering the handle up to the stock.

5. Chop out the mortise to a depth of 20mm.

6. Carefully pare the sides of the mortise to the gauge lines.

7. Fit the handle into the stock but do not glue it in place yet.

POINTS FOR EMPHASIS

○ If the handle is glued in place now it will be difficult to chamfer the stock in the next stage.

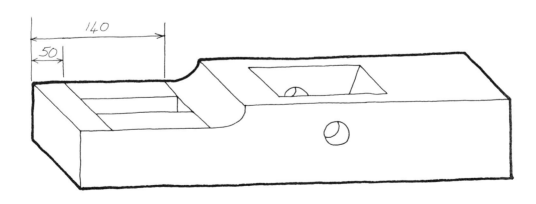

DEMO 13   Chamfering the stock

Why   To make the plane comfortable to hold.

Materials   Workpieces from the last demonstration.

Tools   Jack plane; 25mm chisel; pencil; small tin.

ACTIONS

1. Thumb-gauge a line all round the top of the stock, 4mm from each edge, to mark the chamfers.

2. Mark radiuses on the top, sides, front and back of the stock. A small tin may help to make the curves even.

3. Plane the chamfers down to the pencil lines on both sides. You will have to use a chisel on the curve in the middle of the stock. Then use a wide chisel to round off the corners.

4. The handle can now be glued into position. Use a clamp to push it tightly into the mortise.

POINTS FOR EMPHASIS

o   The appearance of the plane will be improved if the chamfers are even.

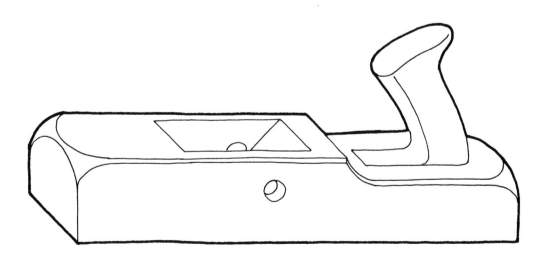

Two-piece jack plane   121

Making the wedge

Why　　　　　The wedge holds the plane blade tightly against the frog of the plane.

Materials　　One piece of hardwood 200 × 50 × 20mm.

Tools　　　　Try-square; ruler; pencil; ripsaw; jack plane; 25mm chisel.

ACTIONS

1. Square a line all round, 100mm from one end, and mark the angle for the wedge. Square another line 130mm from the same end to mark the top of the wedge.

2. Use a ripsaw to cut the angle of the wedge, and plane the sawn face square and smooth.

3. Saw off the end of the wedge with a tenon-saw, and round off the top by paring the end grain with a chisel.

4. Chamfer the thin end of the wedge to allow the shavings to pass over it easily.

POINTS FOR EMPHASIS

○ Radiusing the top of the wedge will prevent it from splitting when struck with a hammer.

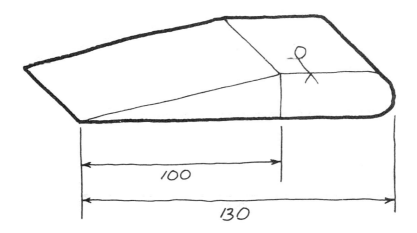

DEMO 15 Fitting the blade

Why   So that the plane will leave a straight, smooth surface with-
                 out becoming choked.

Materials   Plane stock; blade; wedge; crossbar.

Tools   25mm chisel; mallet or hammer; straight edge; jack plane.

ACTIONS

1. If you have bought a blade from a hardware shop it should fit easily into
    the throat and through the mouth.

2. If the blade you are going to use has been made by a blacksmith it may be
    too thick to fit through the mouth. Square a line on the sole, 1mm from the
    front of the mouth, and open it out with a hammer and chisel. Repeat this
    process until there is a gap of about 3–4mm between the front of the blade
    and the front of the mouth.

3. Position the blade so that the cutting edge is about 5mm inside the throat,
    and wedge it tight. Clamp the plane upside down in a vice and plane the
    sole straight and true.

POINTS FOR EMPHASIS

o   Clearance between the blade and the side of the throat allows some lateral
    adjustment.

o   If the mouth is made too big it will leave a rough finish on crossgrain
    timber. If it is too small the plane will become choked when used.

o   The wedge tends to bend the stock of the plane when it is tight, so the sole
    should be trued up when the blade and wedge are in position.

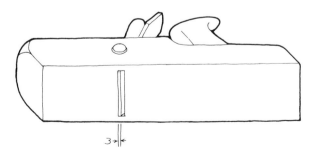

Two-piece jack plane   123

DEMO 16   Setting and using the plane

Why   So that you can become accustomed to adjusting and using
               the plane.

Materials   One piece of scrap timber.

Tools   Finished jack plane; small hammer.

ACTIONS

1. Hold the stock of the plane with one finger underneath the mouth. Put the
    blade into the throat and let it rest on your finger so that it does not project
    below the sole of the plane.

2. Place the wedge between the blade and the crossbar.

3. Tap the wedge gently with a hammer to tighten it.

4. Test the setting.

5. If the plane is not cutting, hit the top of the blade gently and tap the wedge
    to tighten it again.

6. If the plane is cutting too deep, hit the back of the plane to bring back the
    blade, and tap the wedge gently to tighten it again.

7. Look along the bottom of the plane to make sure the cutting edge is
    parallel to the sole. If one corner is too high, tap the opposite side of the
    blade.

8. Repeat these actions until the plane cuts a fine, even shaving.

9. To remove the blade, simply hit the back of the stock until the wedge
    becomes loose.

PLOUGH PLANE

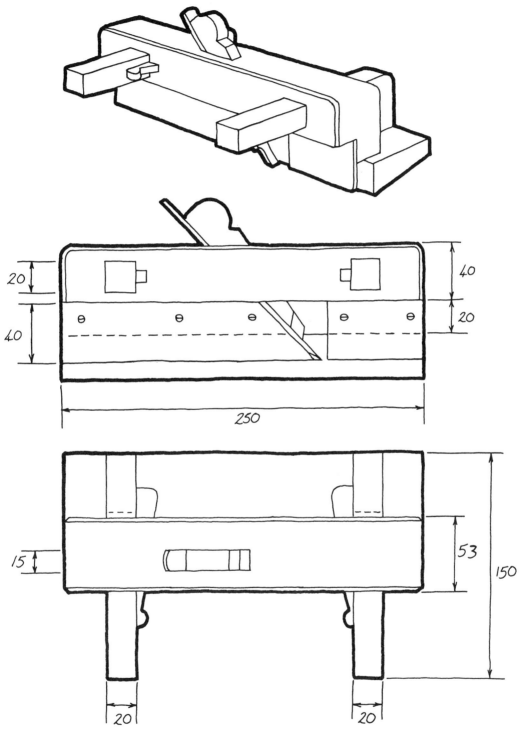

Objective

At the end of this session each participant will have made a plough plane.

Previous knowledge assumed

Competence in: preparing timber, marking out and cutting mortise and tenon joints, drilling pilot and clearance holes for wood-screws.

Tools required

Try-square	Tenon-saw	Mallet
Pencil steel	Hacksaw	45mm and 3mm bit
Jack plane	Scriber	Screwdriver
6mm chisel	Straight edge	Flat file
25mm chisel	Rule or tape measure	Centre punch
Wheel brace	Marking gauge	'G' clamp
Countersink bit	12mm chisel	

Common problems

Fitting the arms into the stock
Making the sole plate
Fitting the sole plate to the stock

Cutting list

The instructor and each student need to prepare hardwood timber to the following dimensions (mm):

ITEM	QUANTITY	MATERIAL	L	W	T
Stock	1	Hardwood	250	40	30
	1	Hardwood	250	60	23
Wedge	1	Hardwood	120	30	15
Fence	1	Hardwood	250	75	30
Arms	2	Hardwood	170	65	20
Keys	2	Hardwood	120	20	15

Also needed

Four 40 × 4mm wood-screws; two 30 × 4mm wood-screws; five 20 × 4mm round-head wood-screws; one mild steel plate 250 × 40 × 3mm; plough plane blade (this will have to be forged from spring steel or ground from an old cutting tool); PVA wood glue.

Introduction

Time   Two days.

What   In this session we are all going to make a wooden plough plane.

Why   Plough planes are used for cutting grooves to let panels into doors, office desks and drawers. They are expensive and difficult to buy in most developing countries.

                The plough plane is probably the most difficult tool to make. It requires the accurate cutting and fitting of a number of wooden components, as well as some metalworking skills.

How   The session will be made up of a series of demonstrations. Each step will be demonstrated two or three times. I will ask some questions to check that the demonstration was clear, then you will practise the same operation. We will wait until everyone is finished before the next step is demonstrated.

This is the plough plane we are going to make. [SHOW TOOL TO TRAINEES] It works like this.

These are the parts.

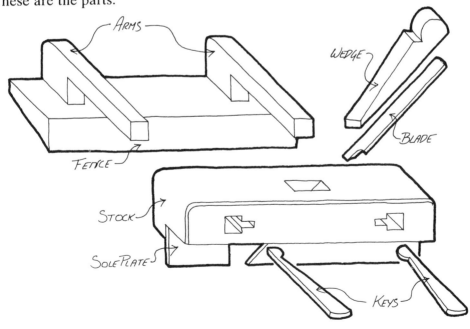

DEMO 1   Marking out the blade and wedge recess

Why   So that the recess can be cut accurately.

Materials   One piece of hardwood 250 × 40 × 30mm.

Tools   Marking gauge; try-square; pencil; tape measure.

ACTIONS

1. Choose and mark the front of the stock; it should point to your left.

2. On the bottom of the piece, square a line 125mm from the front. On the top, square a line 165mm from the front. Join these lines up with a diagonal on the side to mark the angle of the frog.

3. To mark the angle for the wedge, square a line on the bottom of the piece 105mm from the front. On the top, square a line 135mm from the front. Join these lines up with a diagonal on the side.

4. Gauge a line on the top and bottom of the stock, 15mm from the face side, to mark the depth of the recess.

5. Mark the waste.

6. To mark the position of the screws that hold the stock together, square two lines all round, 15mm and 80mm from each end. Gauge a centre line on the face side. The waste can now be removed from the recess.

POINTS FOR EMPHASIS

○ All marking out must be done from the face side or the face edge.

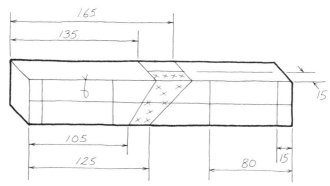

128   *Plough plane*

DEMO 2 Assembling the stock

Why   To form the stock of the plane.

Materials   One piece of hardwood 250 × 60 × 25mm; workpiece from the last demonstration; four 40 × 4mm wood-screws.

Tools   Wheel brace; 4mm and 3mm drill bits; countersink bit; small hammer; screwdriver.

ACTIONS

1. Drill four 4mm clearance holes right through the stock where the pencil and the gauge lines meet.

2. Countersink the holes.

3. Clamp the two parts of the stock together, making sure that the wide opening of the housing is at the top of the stock and that both pieces are correctly aligned.

4. Mark the position of the four 3mm pilot holes in the second piece. Unclamp the pieces and drill the pilot holes.

5. Spread a layer of glue on the face side of the smaller section of the stock.

6. Use four 40 × 4mm wood-screws to fix the two sections securely together. Wipe off any excess glue with a wet rag and leave it to set for three or four hours.

POINTS FOR EMPHASIS

o   Drilling the correct-size clearance and pilot holes is essential, particularly in hardwoods.

o   Ask someone to check that the drill is square.

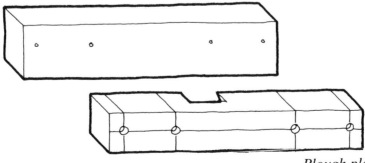

Plough plane   129

DEMO 3   Cleaning up the stock

Why   To give it a new face side and face edge from which to mark
               out the rest of the stock.

Materials   The assembled stock.

Tools   Try-square; pencil; jack plane; 12mm chisel.

ACTIONS

1. Remove any excess glue from the recess with a small chisel.

2. Check that the largest side is straight and flat (correct if necessary) and
    mark it as the face side.

3. Plane the top of the stock straight, square to the face side, and mark it as
    the face edge.

POINTS FOR EMPHASIS

○ Good preparation is necessary if the arms are to be marked out accurately.

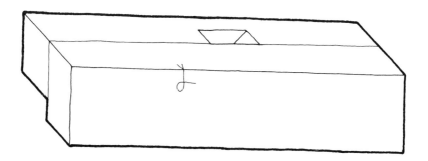

DEMO 4   Cutting the mortises in the stock

Why   So that the arms can pass through the stock.

Materials   Stock assembly.

Tools   Marking gauge; tape measure; 12mm chisel; mallet or
                 hammer.

ACTIONS

1. Mark out the stock as shown in the drawing.

2. Use a 12mm chisel to chop out the mortises. The chisel must be used
   across the grain. Leave 1mm or 2mm all round the mortises to be cleaned
   up at the end. Cut halfway through from one side, turn the workpiece over
   and finish cutting from the other side.

3. Check that the insides of the mortises are straight.

POINTS FOR EMPHASIS

o All marking out must be done from the face side.
o The position of the arms must be marked accurately on both pieces.
o Leave 1mm or 2mm all round the mortises to be cleaned up when the joint
   has been cut right through.

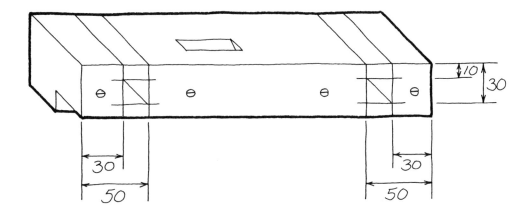

Plough plane 131

DEMO 5 Cutting the stopped housings in the fence

Why   So that the arms can be jointed to the fence.

Materials   Stock; fence bottom.

Tools   Marking gauge; try-squre; pencil; tape measure or ruler; 25mm chisel; 12mm chisel; mallet or hammer.

ACTIONS

1. Continue squaring the previously marked lines on the face side and face edge of the fence, and mark it out as shown in the drawing.

2. Take a wide chisel. With the bevel of the blade facing the middle of the joint, drive it straight down with a hammer, a few millimetres from the pencil line. Remove a wedge of waste and repeat until you reach the middle. Do the same at the other side of the joint. Then pare carefully back to the pencil lines.

3. With a smaller chisel, clean up the bottom of the housings and the stopped ends.

POINTS FOR EMPHASIS

o All marking out must be done from the face side or the face edge.
o Leave pencil lines showing when the joint is cut.

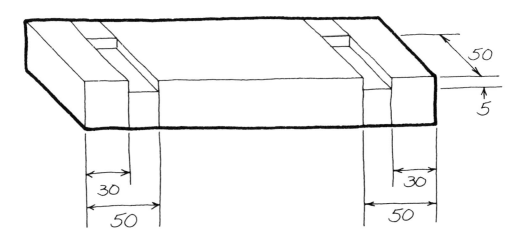

DEMO 6   Making the arms

Why   The arms connect the stock of the plane to the fence.

Materials   Two pieces of hardwood 170 × 65 × 20mm.

Tools   Marking gauge; try-squre; pencil; jack plane; 25mm chisel; ripsaw; tenon-saw.

ACTIONS

1. Square a line all round, 50mm from one end. This marks the length of the shoulder.

2. Set a gauge to 20mm and gauge both sides up to the pencil line. This marks the width of the arm.

3. Remove the waste with a tenon-saw or a handsaw.

4. Clean up the sawn edges by carefully paring away the waste with a chisel. The inside corner can be finished by scraping.

POINTS FOR EMPHASIS

o   Saw on the waste side of the line.
o   Take care to follow the grain when paring away the waste.

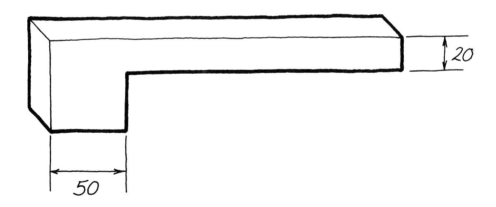

Plough plane   133

DEMO 7   Assembling the fence

Why   So that the arms are firmly fixed to the fence.

Materials   Workpieces from the last demonstration; fence bottom; two
                30 × 4mm wood-screws.

Tools   Wheel brace; 3mm twist bit; 4mm twist bit; countersink bit
                (if available); screwdriver.

ACTIONS

1. Fit the arms into the fence and mark the respective joints.

2. Drill two 4mm clearance holes through the fence into the housing, about
   25mm from the face edge.

3. Countersink the holes.

4. Assemble the fence. Mark the position of the screws in the arms and drill
   two 3mm pilot holes.

5. Spread a layer of glue into the housing joint and screw the fence tightly
   together.

6. Push the arms through the stock and allow the glue to dry for a few hours.

POINTS FOR EMPHASIS

o   Drilling the correct-size clearance and pilot holes is essential, particularly
    in hardwoods.
o   Allowing the glue to set while the arms are positioned in the stock will help
    to align the arms correctly.

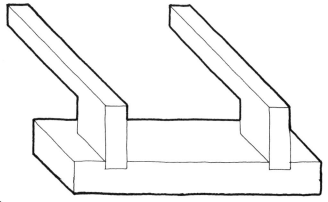

DEMO 8 Cutting the housings in the stock for the keys

Why So that the wedges can be fitted into the stock.

Materials The stock of the plough plane.

Tools Try-square; marking gauge; tape measure; pencil; 6mm chisel; mallet or hammer.

ACTIONS

1. On the face side, square a line 15mm from the mortise towards the middle of the stock. On the other side, square a line 10mm from the mortise towards the middle of the stock. These different dimensions allow for the taper in the wedge.

2. Gauge two 10mm-wide housings, centred on the mortises, up to the pencil lines.

3. Mark the waste.

4. Chisel down from both sides at an angle so that they meet in the middle of the mortise.

5. Turn the stock over so that the big side of the recess is on the top; cut carefully until the end of the recess is straight and meets the pencil lines on both sides.

POINTS FOR EMPHASIS

○ All marking out must be done from the face side or the face edge.
○ Remove the waste a little at a time.

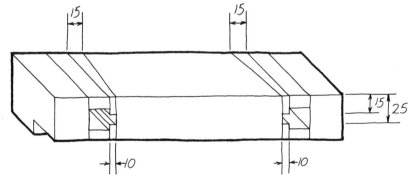

Plough plane 135

DEMO 9   Making the keys

Why   The keys hold the fence in the required position.

Materials   One piece of hardwood $120 \times 20 \times 10$mm.

Tools   Try-square; tape measure; pencil; tenon-saw; 12mm chisel.

ACTIONS

1. Draw a diagonal line from one corner of the workpiece to 5mm above the other corner.

2. Mark a knob 10mm from the small end. This will prevent the wedge from falling out of the stock.

3. Use a tenon-saw to remove the bulk of the waste. Place the wedge on a bench hook to cut down behind the knob.

4. Carefully pare the wedge down, holding it against the stop of the bench hook.

5. Round off the end with a chisel and some sandpaper.

6. To fit the keys, push them through the housings in the stock and push the arms of the fence through the mortises. Drive the keys gently into the housings and check that there are no gaps between them and the stock.

POINTS FOR EMPHASIS

o   Take care not to split the knob from the wedge.
o   There should be no gaps between the wedge and the stock; otherwise the wedge will not grip tightly.

DEMO 10 Chamfering the stock

Why   To make the plane comfortable to hold.

Materials Stock assemblies; fence assemblies.

Tools   25mm chisel; pencil; jack plane; a coin.

ACTIONS

1. Mark radiuses on the sides of the stock at the top of both ends, using a pencil and a coin.

2. Pare the corners back to the radius with a 25mm chisel.

3. Thumb-gauge lines, 4mm from each edge, on the front, top and back. Do not mark the bottom of the stock.

4. Plane the straight chamfers down to the pencil lines and work the curved chamfers with a chisel.

5. Mark a radius on the back edges of the arms, using a pencil and a coin. Pare the corners back to the pencil line.

POINTS FOR EMPHASIS

o The edges of the fence should be kept square, to allow good contact with the workpiece.
o The appearance of the plane will be improved if the chamfers are even.

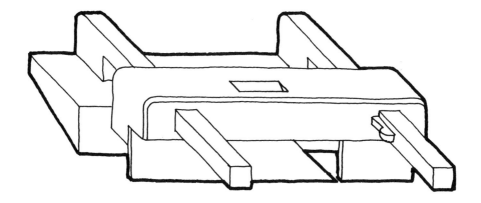

DEMO 11   Marking out the sole plate

Why   The sole plate allows the blade to project into the groove.

Materials   One piece of mild steel plate 250 × 40 × 3mm.

Tools   Tape measure; try-square; straight edge; file; centre punch; scriber or broken hacksaw blade.

ACTIONS

1. Prepare a piece of 3mm-thick mild steel plate by cutting and filing it to 250 × 40mm. Make sure the edges are straight and the corners are square.

2. Mark out the sole plate as in the drawing, using a scriber or broken piece of hacksaw blade to draw the lines. The positions of the screw holes are marked by the crossing lines, and the diagonal line marks the angle of the blade.

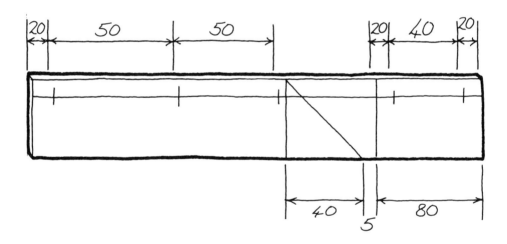

DEMO 12 Cutting and drilling the sole plate

Why   So that the sole plate can be attached to the stock.

Materials   Workpiece from last demonstration.

Tools   Wheel brace; hacksaw; try-square; centre punch file; 4mm drill bit.

ACTIONS

1. Use a centre punch to dent the centre of each hole before drilling.

2. Use a wheel brace and a 4mm drill bit to bore the holes.

3. Use a hacksaw to cut away the waste section of the sole plate.

4. Check that the angle of the sole plate is the same as the angle of the frog.

POINTS FOR EMPHASIS

o   Masonry nails can often be used instead of a centre punch.
o   A drop of oil will make the drilling easier.
o   Protect wooden vice jaws from damage with some scrap wood.
o   The angle on the sole plate must be the same as the angle of the frog so that the blade is supported as close to the cutting edge as possible.

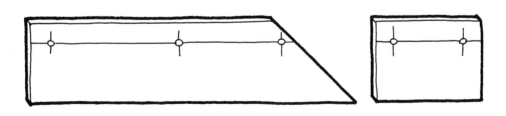

DEMO 13   Fitting the sole plate

Materials   One piece of cardboard 250 × 20mm; five 20 × 4mm wood-
screws; stock assembly; sole plate.

Tools   Wheel brace; 3mm drill bit; screwdriver; 'G' clamp.

ACTIONS

1. Clamp the two parts of the sole plate onto the stock, making sure that the frog follows a straight line.

2. Drill five 3mm pilot holes into the stock of the plane.

3. Cut a piece of cardboard about 250mm long and 20mm wide. This must be placed between the sole plate and the stock.

4. Unclamp the sole plate. Place the cardboard between it and the stock and screw the sole plate to the stock.

5. Cut the cardboard away from the throat of the plane.

POINTS FOR EMPHASIS

o The cardboard is needed to give the cutting edge clearance in the side of the groove it cuts (similar to the set on the teeth of a handsaw).

o It is essential for the pilot holes to be the correct size, particularly in hardwood.

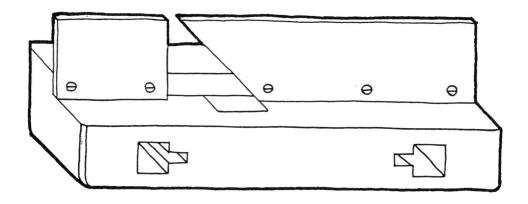

Making the wedge

Why   The wedge holds the blade firmly in position.

Materials   One piece of hardwood 120 × 30 × 15mm.

Tools   Tape measure; ruler; straight edge; jack plane; tenon-saw; 25mm chisel.

ACTIONS

1. Mark the wedge out 30mm wide at one end and 5mm at the other. Mark out a rounded head at the top of the wedge.

2. Saw the wedge with a tenon-saw and plane the sawn face.

3. Cut the shoulder at the head of the wedge with a tenon-saw.

4. Use a chisel to pare away the corners at the top of the wedge.

POINTS FOR EMPHASIS

o It is useful to be able to hit the rounded head from the front of the plane to loosen the blade.

DEMO 15   Fitting the wedge

Why   The bottom of the wedge helps to eject the shavings from the throat of the plane.

Materials   Workpiece from the last demonstration; plough plane blade.

Tools   Pencil; tenon-saw.

ACTIONS

1. Take the blade you are going to use.

2. Fit the wedge and the blade into the stock and plane the wedge to fit. Check that there are no gaps.

3. Draw in, freehand, the double angle at the bottom of the wedge. The very end of the wedge should be level with the bottom section of the stock.

4. Saw the tip of the wedge off with a tenon-saw.

POINTS FOR EMPHASIS

o   The wedge must fit well to hold the blade tightly in position.

DEMO 16   Setting and using the plough plane

Why   So that you are able to cut grooves in timber.

Materials   Completed plough plane and blade; one piece of scrap wood, planed face side and face edge.

Tools   Ruler; mallet; bench and vice.

ACTIONS

1. Place the blade and the wedge into the plane and tighten the wedge gently with a mallet.

2. Assemble the plane by placing the keys into the housings and the fence arms into the mortises. A little candle wax on the arms will make them slide easily.

3. Set the fence to the required distance and tighten the keys with your thumbs. Check the distance between the sole plate and the fence is the same at the front and back of the plane, and make any adjustments.

4. Tighten the keys securely by hitting them gently with a hammer or a small piece of wood, and check the setting again.

5. Test the setting of the blade. Clamp a piece of wood into your vice. Press the plane down onto the edge of the timber and the fence against the side of it and push the plane along the length of the timber.

6. If the plane is cutting too deep, hit the back of the plane to bring back the blade, and tap the wedge gently to tighten it again.

7. If the plane does not cut, hit the top of the blade gently and tap the wedge to tighten it again. Repeat these actions until the plane cuts a fine, even shaving.

8. Once you have adjusted the blade you can begin ploughing a groove. Start cutting about 100m from the far end of the workpiece. Take longer and longer cuts until the groove runs the full length of the timber. Then plane the groove down to the desired depth.

9. To remove the blade, hit the back of the stock or the front of the wedge until the blade becomes loose.

WORKBENCH AND VICE

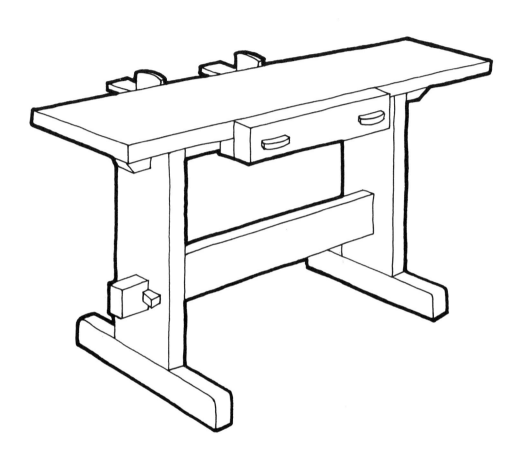

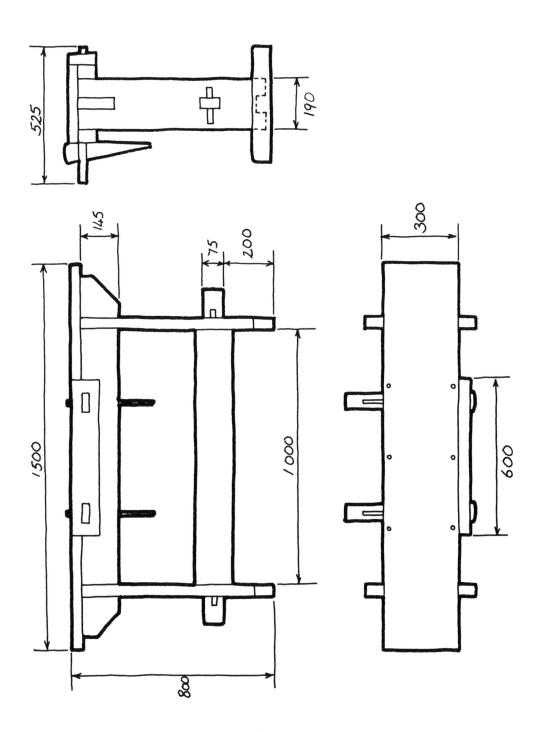

Objective

At the end of this session each participant will have made a workbench and vice.

Previous knowledge assumed

Competence in: preparing timber, marking out and cutting mortise and tenon joints, bridle joints, housing joints, and drilling pilot and clearance holes for wood-screws.

Tools required

Try-square	Wheel brace	25mm chisel
Steel rule or tape measure	Screwdriver	Tenon-saw
Marking gauge	Carpenters' brace	4mm and 3mm drill bits
20mm chisel	Pencil	Two sash clamps
Ripsaw	Jack plane	12mm auger bit
Mallet	6mm chisel	

Common problems

Cutting the dovetail mortises in the jaw
Cutting the dovetails in the arms
Selecting poor quality wood for the wedges

Cutting list

The instructor and each student need to prepare hardwood timber to the following dimensions (mm):

ITEM	QUANTITY	MATERIAL	L	W	T
Bench top	1	Hardwood	1500	300	45
Legs	2	Softwood	755	190	45
Top rail	1	Softwood	1400	145	45
Bottom rail	1	Softwood	1300	145	45
Bench wedges	1	Hardwood	150	30	15
Feet	2	Softwood	450	70	45
Battens	2	Softwood	200	50	25
Arms	2	Hardwood	525	75	25
Vice wedges	1	Hardwood	400	100	15
Guide rails	2	Hardwood	600	70	45
Jaw	1	Hardwood	600	115	45

Also needed

Six 12 × 125mm nuts, bolts and washers
Six 50 × 4mm wood-screws

Introduction

Time   Four days.

What   We are going to make a simple workbench and vice.

Why   All carpenters need some kind of bench to work at, but often those working in developing countries are only able to afford a large wooden plank nailed to the trunk of a tree. The bench we are going to make will also consist of a single plank top, but with the addition of a simple but effective wooden vice. A vice is essential if wooden tools are going to be manufactured.

How   The session will be made up of a series of demonstrations. Each step will be demonstrated two or three times. I will ask some questions to check that the demonstration was clear, then you will wait until everyone is finished before the next step is demonstrated.

This is the bench we are going to make. [SHOW THE BENCH TO TRAINEES] It works like this.

These are the parts.

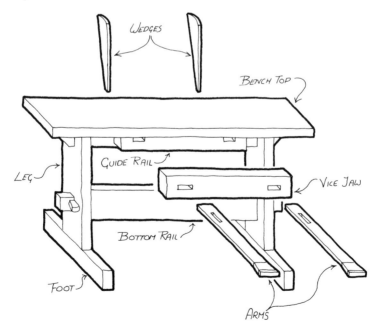

Workbench and vice 147

DEMO 1   Marking out the legs

Why   So that the joints can be cut.

Materials   Two pieces of 755 × 190 × 45mm softwood.

Tools   Tape measure; try-square; marking gauge.

ACTIONS

1. Square a line all round 145mm from the top of the legs. Gauge a 20mm-wide socket in the middle of both sides. This marks the bridle joint for the top rail.

2. Square two lines, 200mm and 275mm from the bottom of the legs.

3. Gauge a 45mm-wide mortise in the centre of both sides. This marks the through mortise for the bottom rail.

4. Square a line all round 60mm from the bottom of the leg to mark the length of the tenon that joins the legs to the feet.

POINTS FOR EMPHASIS

o   All marking out must be done from the face side or the face edge.

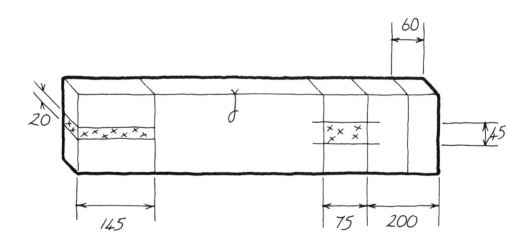

DEMO 2   Marking out the mortises in the feet

Why   So that the joints can be cut.

Materials Workpieces from the last demonstration; two pieces of 450 × 70 × 45mm softwood.

Tools   Ruler; try-square; mortise gauge; pencil.

ACTIONS

1. Square a line across the middle of the face edge of both feet.

2. Square two lines, 30mm either side of this mark, to mark the haunch in the centre of the tenon.

3. Square another two lines, 95mm either side of the centre mark, to mark the full width of the tenons.

4. Set a mortise gauge to mark a 15mm mortise in the centre of the feet.

5. Gauge the tenons on the legs using the same gauge setting. If you have only a marking gauge, set it first to 15mm and then to 30mm.

6. Mark the waste.

POINTS FOR EMPHASIS

o All marking out must be done from the face side or the face edge.

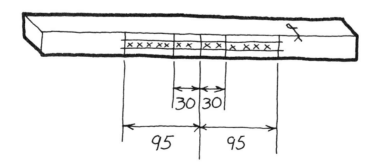

DEMO 3   Marking out the top and bottom rails

Why   So that the joints can be cut.

Materials   One piece of 1400 × 145 × 45mm softwood (top rail); one piece of 1300 × 145 × 45mm softwood (bottom rail).

Tools   Ruler; try-square; marking gauge.

ACTIONS

1. Hold or clamp the two rails together so that the top rail overhangs the bottom rail by 50mm at both ends.

2. Square two lines across the edge of both pieces, 1000mm apart at equal distances from both ends.

3. Mark out the bottom rail as shown in the drawing.

4. Check that you have marked out the joint correctly by measuring the rail up against the legs.

5. Mark the width of the housing in the top rail by squaring two lines all round, 45mm from the first line in both directions. Gauge the depth of the housings by setting a gauge first to 12.5mm and then to 32.5mm.

6. Check that you have marked out the joint correctly as before.

7. Mark the waste.

POINTS FOR EMPHASIS

○ All marking out must be done from the face side or the face edge.

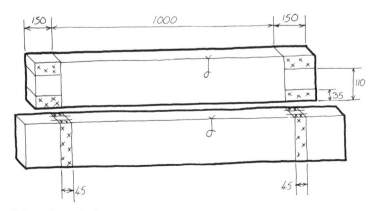

150 *Workbench and vice*

DEMO 4   Cutting the joints in the legs

Why   So that the legs can be fixed to the feet and the rails.

Materials   The two legs.

Tools   Ripsaw; tenon-saw; 20mm chisel; mallet or hammer.

ACTIONS

1. Saw down the sides of the socket at the top of the legs with a ripsaw.

2. Chop out the waste with a mallet and chisel. Place the cutting edge on the pencil line with the bevel facing the end of the leg. Drive the chisel straight down, and remove a chip from the waste side. Continue until you cut halfway through. Turn the leg over and finish cutting from the other side.

3. Chop out the through mortises at the bottom of the legs. Again, cut halfway through from one side, turn the leg over and finish the mortise from the other side.

4. Use a ripsaw to cut the cheeks of the tenon.

5. Cut the shoulder of the tenon with a tenon-saw.

POINTS FOR EMPHASIS

o   Always saw on the waste side of the lines.

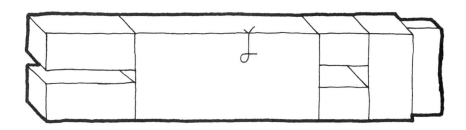

DEMO 5   Cutting the joints in the feet

Why   So that the feet can be fixed to the legs.

Materials   The two feet.

Tools   Mortise chisel; 25mm chisel; mallet or hammer.

ACTIONS

1. Chop out the mortises at the end of the joints to a depth of 40mm.

2. Cut the groove for the central haunch to a depth of 10mm.

3. Mark the position and depth of the haunch on the tenon. To remove the waste, saw down the side of the tenon and chop out the haunch with a chisel.

4. Fit the joint, then glue and clamp it up.

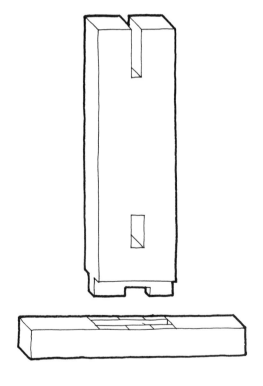

DEMO 6   Cutting the joints in the bottom rail

Why　　　　　So that the bottom rail can be fixed to the legs.

Materials　　Two pieces of hardwood 150 × 30 × 15mm (wedges); the bottom rail.

Tools　　　　Ripsaw; tenon-saw; try-square; marking gauge; ruler or tape measure; pencil.

ACTIONS

1. Use a ripsaw to cut the cheeks of the tenons at both ends.

2. Cut the shoulders with a tenon-saw.

3. Mark out and cut a tapered through mortise in the centre of each tenon, to take the wedge. The mortise should be 15mm wide, 20mm long on one side and 15mm long on the other. It should start 40mm from the shoulder of the tenon.

4. Fit the rail into the mortises in the legs.

5. Take the two 150 × 30 × 15mm pieces prepared for the wedges and plane them to fit into the tapered mortises.

6. Drive the wedges in tight to secure the joint.

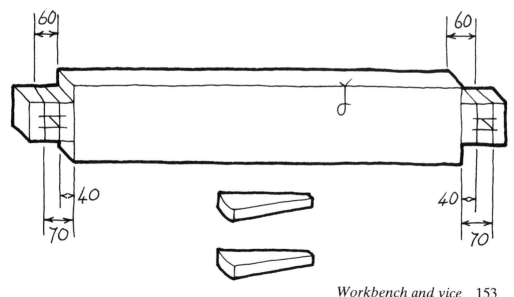

Workbench and vice   153

DEMO 7   Cutting the joints in the top rail

Why   So that the rail can be jointed to the legs. The four sockets
                         cut in the top of the rail allow the bench top to be fixed to the
                         rail and the arms of the vice to slide under the top.

Materials   The top rail.

Tools   Tenon-saw; 25mm chisel; tape measure; try-square; marking
                         gauge; pencil.

ACTIONS

1. Saw down the sides of the housing joints with a tenon-saw and make one
    or two saw cuts in the waste.

2. Chop out the housing down to the gauge line with a wide chisel. Fit the rail
    into the housings in the legs.

3. Square a centre line across the top of the rail and mark two housings,
    175mm either side of this line, 75mm long. (These allow the arms of the
    vice to pass under the bench.)

4. Mark two housings, 50mm long, 350mm either side of the centre line
    (these take the battens which fix the top rail to the bench top).

5. Set a gauge to 25mm and gauge the depth of all four joints.

6. Saw down the sides of the housings and remove the waste with a wide
    chisel.

7. Mark and cut a mitre on the bottom of the rail and plane the sawn face
    smooth.

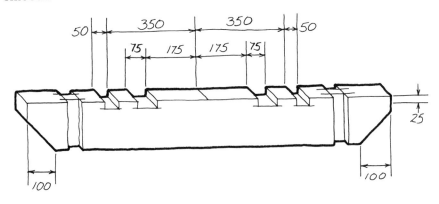

DEMO 8 Fitting the battens and the bench top

Why

So that the bench top can be fixed to the top rail.

Materials

Two pieces of 200 × 50 × 25mm softwood; two 50 × 4mm wood-screws; wood glue.

Tools

Try-square; marking gauge; pencil; wheel brace; 4mm twist bit; 3mm twist bit; screwdriver.

ACTIONS

1. Gauge a line down the centre of both pieces. Square a line across the middle, and two lines 75mm either side of the centre line.

2. Drill six 4mm clearance holes where the lines meet. Countersink the outside holes on one side and the central holes on the other side.

3. Glue and screw the battens to the outside housings on the top of the rail.

4. Screw the battens to the bottom of the bench top, making sure it overhangs evenly on all sides.

5. Now slot the top rail into the sockets in the legs and the bench is complete.

POINTS FOR EMPHASIS

o It is essential that the clearance and pilot holes are the correct size, particularly in hardwoods.
o Chamfering all exposed edges will prevent splintering.

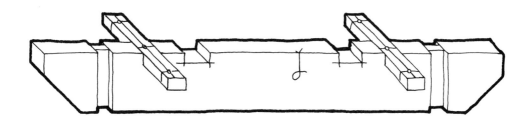

Workbench and vice 155

DEMO 9   Cutting the housings in the guide rails

Why   The housings guide the arms of the vice.

Materials   Two pieces of 600 × 70 × 45mm hardwood.

Tools   Try-square; marking gauge; tape measure; pencil; tenon-saw; 25mm chisel; mallet or hammer.

ACTIONS

1. Square a centre line across the face edge; then square lines all round, 180mm and 245mm either side of the centre line. Set a marking gauge to 26mm and gauge the depth of the housing.

2. Saw down the sides of the housing with a tenon-saw and make two or three cuts in the waste.

3. Remove the waste with a wide chisel and check that the bottom of the housing is straight.

POINTS FOR EMPHASIS

o   Gauging the depth of the housings at 26mm gives clearance for 25mm-thick arms.

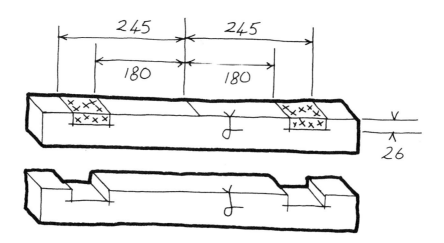

DEMO 10 Marking out the jaw

Why   So that the joints can be cut.

Materials   One piece of hardwood 600 × 115 × 45mm.

Tools   Try-square; marking gauge; tape measure; pencil.

ACTIONS

1. To mark the position of the through mortise, first square a centre line across the face edge. Then square lines all round, 180mm and 245mm either side of the centre line.

2. On the face side, square a line 5mm either side of the mortise. This marks the taper for the dovetails in the end of the arms.

3. Mark a 25mm-wide through mortise in the jaw for the arms. The top of the mortise should be 45mm from the top of the jaw (the same thickness as the bench top), so gauge the mortises first at 45mm and then at 70mm.

POINTS FOR EMPHASIS

o All marking out must be done from the face side or the face edge.
o It is important that the top of the vice is level with the top of the jaw.

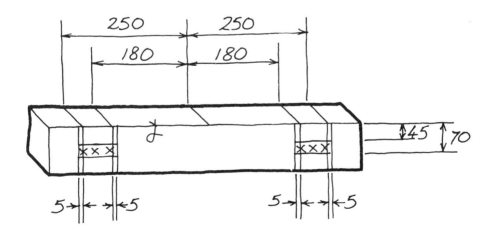

DEMO 11 Cutting the mortises in the jaw

Why   So that the arms can be fitted to the jaw.

Materials   Workpiece from the last demonstration.

Tools   20mm chisel; mallet or hammer; pencil; jack plane.

ACTIONS

1. To chop out the mortises, cut halfway through from one side, turn the jaw over and cut right through from the other, leaving a few millimetres of waste before the line.

2. Carefully cut the tapered ends of the mortise.

3. Thumb-gauge lines all round each face, 4mm from the edge.

4. Plane the chamfers down to the pencil lines.

POINTS FOR EMPHASIS

○ Leave 1mm or 2mm all round the mortise to be cleaned up when the joint has been cut right through.
○ Chamfering the jaw will prevent splinters.

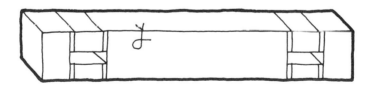

DEMO 12   Marking out the arms

Why   So that the joints can be cut.

Materials   Two pieces of hardwood 525 × 75 × 25mm.

Tools   Try-square; mortise gauge; tape measure.

ACTIONS

1. Square lines all round, 20mm and 65mm from one end. This marks the length of the dovetail.

2. Gauge a line 5mm from both edges on both sides, and mark in the angle of the dovetail between the two pencil lines.

3. The mortise at the back of the arm needs to be the same distance from the dovetail as the width of the bench top, plus an extra 15mm. (If your top is 300mm wide then this measurement should be 315mm.)

4. The through mortise should be 75mm long and 15mm wide. Gauge it in the centre of the arm.

5. On the face side add an extra 3mm to the length of the mortise.

POINTS FOR EMPHASIS

○ The extra 15mm between the dovetail and the mortise for the wedge gives the vice a bigger capacity.
○ The angle at the back of the mortise in the arm allows for the taper in the wedge.

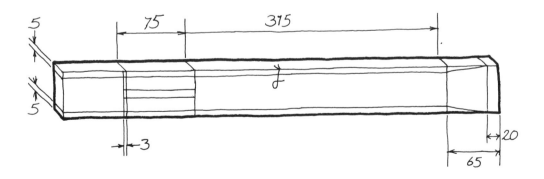

Workbench and vice   159

DEMO 13   Cutting the joints in the arms

Why   So that the arms can be fitted to the jaw.

Materials   Workpieces from the last demonstration.

Tools   Jack plane; ripsaw; 25mm chisel; 12mm chisel; mallet or
                   hammer.

ACTIONS

1. Clamp the arm in the vice and saw right down to the dovetail.

2. Carefully pare the angle of the dovetail with a wide chisel.

3. Plane as much of the sawn face as smooth as you can, and scrape the rest
    down to the gauge line with a plane blade or scraper.

4. Chop out the mortises. Cut halfway through from one side, turn the arm
    over and cut right through from the other side, leaving a few millimetres of
    waste before the line. Clean up the ends of the mortise, remembering to
    pare the angle at the back.

5. Radius the front of the arms by paring straight down with a wide chisel.

6. Fit the arms into the jaw with the face side up. Check that the dovetails are
    tight.

POINTS FOR EMPHASIS

○ Saw on the waste side of the lines.
○ Leave 1mm or 2mm all round the mortise to be cleaned up when the joint
   has been cut right through.

DEMO 14   Making the wedges

Why   When driven down, the wedges pull the jaw of the vice into
                 the bench and will clamp the workpiece in position.

Materials   One piece of hardwood 400 × 100 × 15mm (two wedges can
                 be made from this size of timber).

Tools   Tape measure; straight edge; ripsaw; jack plane.

ACTIONS

1. At one end of the piece, mark a point 10mm in from the edge: on the other
    end, mark another point 10mm in from the opposite edge. Join these
    points up with a diagonal line.

2. Use a handsaw to rip down the centre of the line, and plane the sawn edge
    straight and square.

3. Mark a radius at the top of each wedge with a pencil and a tin, or similar
    object, about 150mm in diameter.

4. Cut and smooth the radius down to the pencil line, and chamfer the top
    edges.

5. Fit the wedges into the arms.

POINTS FOR EMPHASIS

o The radiused and chamfered ends prevent the wedge from splitting when
   struck with a mallet.

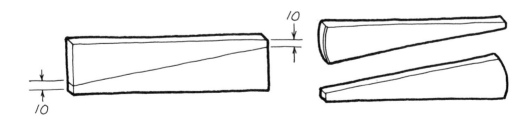

DEMO 15 Marking the bolt holes in the bench top

Why   So that the guide rails can be bolted into position.

Materials   The finished bench.

Tools   Try-square; marking gauge; tape measure, pencil.

ACTIONS

1. Remove the top from the frame of the bench.

2. Square a centre line across the face of the top and two lines all round, 300mm either side of this line. The guide rails fit between the two outside lines.

3. Square two more lines, 275mm either side of the centre line.

4. Gauge points across the inner pencil lines, 22mm in from each edge. These mark the centre of the bolt holes.

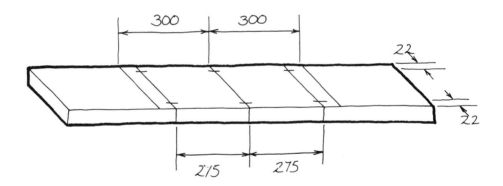

DEMO 16   Fitting the guide rails

Why   So that the vice can be fitted to the bench top.

Materials   Workpieces from the last demonstration; guide rails; six 12 ×
                 125mm nuts, bolts and washers.

Tools   Carpenters' brace; 12mm auger bit; 6mm chisel; mallet or
                 hammer.

ACTIONS

1. Use a brace and a 12mm bit to bore right through the bench. Drill halfway
    through from one side, turn the top over and finish from the other side.

2. Push one of the bolts into each hole in turn, and draw round the head.
    Chop out a six-sided housing for the head of the bolt with a small chisel.

3. Clamp the guide rails in position. They should be between the two outside
    pencil lines and flush with the edge of the bench top.

4. Push the drill through the bench top and drill into the guide rails until the
    centre of the bit appears on the bottom of the rail. Turn the top over and
    finish the holes from the bottom.

5. Bolt the rails tightly into position.

6. Fit the arms into the housings and push the wedges into the mortises at the
    back.

7. The top can now be fitted to the frame of the bench.

POINTS FOR EMPHASIS

o   The drill should be the same diameter as the bolts.
o   The guide rails must be flush with the side of the bench.
o   The heads of the bolts must be below the top of the bench.

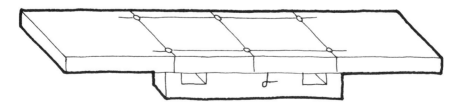

DEMO 17 Using the bench

Why   So that you are able to clamp workpieces in the vice effectively.

Materials   Scrap timber.

Tools   Completed workbench and vice; mallet.

ACTIONS

1. Remove the wedges from the back of the arms.

2. Place a piece of timber between the jaw and the edge of the bench. You can hold it in place by closing the vice with your hip. To tighten the vice, push the wedges into the mortises and hit them with the palm of your hand.

3. To undo the vice, simply pull the wedges out with your hands or hit the small end of the wedge from underneath the bench with a mallet.

POINTS FOR EMPHASIS

o It should not be necessary to use the mallet with force.
o Rub candle wax onto the arms to make them slide easily.

Appendix: Forge work

Introduction to blacksmithing

Objective

At the end of this session each participant will know how to:

1. Work safely in the forge
2. Light a forge fire
3. Maintain a forge fire
4. Use a cold set
5. Draw down a square point
6. Draw down a round point
7. Use top and bottom fullers
8. Bend a tight curve
9. Upset a piece of metal
10. Cut with a hot set
11. Adjust a pair of tongs
12. Harden and temper a piece of carbon steel

Previous knowledge assumed

None

Tools required

Blacksmiths' hearth and anvil
Rake and poker
Sledgehammer
Hand-hammer
Cold set

Hot set
Top and bottom fullers
Flatter
Round mouth tongs
Flat mouth tongs

Materials required

12mm mild steel rod
25 × 12mm flat bar
One piece heavy section bar

Common problems

Maintaining the fire
Quenching the hot set
Cutting on the anvil face

Use of the sledgehammer
Burning the metal
Burning oneself

Introduction

Time   One day.

What   In this session we are going to practise some of the basic forging operations.

Why   You must be familiar with these operations before you can start making even the simplest tools.

How   The session will be made up of short talks and a series of demonstrations. Each operation will be demonstrated two or three times. I will be asking questions to check that the demonstrations and explanations are clear, then you will practise the same operation. We will wait until everyone is finished before the next step is demonstrated.

These are some of the things we are going to practise [SHOW SAMPLES TO TRAINEES].

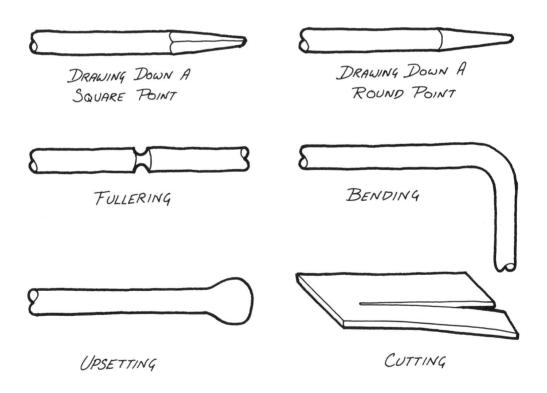

DRAWING DOWN A
SQUARE POINT

DRAWING DOWN A
ROUND POINT

FULLERING

BENDING

UPSETTING

CUTTING

Workshop lesson: Safety

A blacksmiths' workshop can be a safe place to work, but remember that steel worked in this manner needs to be over 800°C and so a number of safety precautions must be observed at all times.

o   Never pick up a piece of metal with your hands before checking the temperature. Test the temperature by placing the palm of your hand a few centimetres above the metal object and feeling for radiated heat. Metal remains a dark grey colour until it is heated to 600°C when it turns a dull red – NEVER ASSUME THAT METAL IS COLD.
o   Only one person at a time should work at the hearth or on the anvil.
o   Check regularly that all hammer heads are securely fixed to their shafts.
o   Always put discarded hot metal in a place where it cannot cause harm.
o   When using tongs, make sure they hold the workpiece securely.
o   The workshop floor should be kept clean.
o   Do not wear clothes that can trap hot pieces of metal such as turn-ups or long boots.
o   Never leave tools, such as sets or fullers, in the anvil, as these can cause injuries when forging with a hand-hammer.

To light the fire

1.   Clear the depression of clinker and partly burnt fuel.

2.   Check blast pipe is clear.

3.   Make a mound of fresh fuel behind the fire.

4.   Fill the depression with paper and kindling.

5.   Light the kindling and, when it is burning well, cover it with fresh fuel.

6.   Leave the fire with a moderate supply of air for 5–10 minutes until it is ready to use.

Maintaining the fire

○ Fuel is expensive. The less fuel used the cheaper the product, or the greater the profit. Cut the air supply every time you remove metal from the fire.

○ Every time you replace your metal, add fresh fuel to the fire.

○ The bottom of the fire will oxidize your workpiece (turn the surface into iron oxide). The top of the fire will reduce your workpiece. Keep the piece of metal you are working on in the top part of the fire and always cover it with fresh fuel.

○ Do not disturb the bed of the fire, and try not to fill it with dirt or dust.

○ Clinker is formed from the impurities in the fuel and must be removed regularly to keep the fire clean.

○ New fuel should be kept behind the fire to allow it to dry and warm up.

Working in the forge

○ Speed is important.

○ All tools must be within easy reach.

○ Keep the anvil clean and dry.

DEMO 1   Using a cold set

Why   This method is quicker and cheaper than using a hacksaw, and is useful when the rod is too long to be put in the fire.

Materials   One length of 12mm rod.

Tools   Cold set; sledgehammer; chalk.

ACTIONS

1. Show cold set to trainees.

2. Measure 800mm from one end of the rod and mark it with chalk.

3. Place rod on cutting block of the anvil.

4. Position the cold set on the mark.

5. Ask trainee to strike the cold set with a sledgehammer.

6. Cut halfway through and bend the rod until it breaks.

POINTS FOR EMPHASIS

o   The cold set must not be used on hot metal as the heat will draw the temper, and make it soft.
o   Do not cut on the face of the anvil as it may become marked.
o   Do not cut right through.

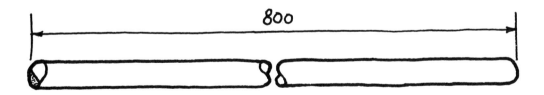

DEMO 2   Drawing down to a square point

Why   This is one of the most important forging operations.

Materials   Workpiece from the last demonstration.

Tools   Hand-hammer.

ACTIONS

1. Heat the first 80mm of the rod up to a yellow heat.

2. Place the end of the rod over the edge of the anvil and lift it up at a slight angle.

3. Start at the tip and forge it down to a short, sharp point, turning it through 90 degrees every two or three blows. Bring the face of the hammer down at a slight angle.

4. Work the taper back until it is 50mm long.

5. Forge it straight and even.

POINTS FOR EMPHASIS

o   Do not let the metal become too hot and melt.
o   The anvil forms one face of the point, while the hammer forms the other.
o   Hold the workpiece near the edge of the anvil so that the hammer can be brought down at an angle without hitting the face of the anvil. If the full length is forged at the beginning, the point will be too long.

DEMO 3   Drawing down to a round point

Why   This is a continuation of the last operation.

Materials   Workpiece from the last demonstration.

Tools   Forging hammer.

ACTIONS

1. Heat the end of the rod up to a yellow heat.

2. Place the rod near the edge of the anvil and lift it up at a slight angle. Twist the rod so that the faces are at 45 degrees to the anvil.

3. Forge in the corners to form an even-sided octagon.

4. Use light hammer blows to forge the point to a round cross-section. Twist the rod continually while using light hammer blows.

5. Straighten up the point.

POINTS FOR EMPHASIS

o Do not let the metal become too hot and melt.
o The anvil forms one face of the point, while the hammer forms the other.
o Hold the workpiece near the edge of the anvil so the hammer can be brought down at an angle without hitting the face of the anvil.
o Whenever a piece of metal is drawn down into a round cross-section it must be forged square first.

DEMO 4 Using top and bottom fullers

Why   This technique will be used to form the necks on the chisels
               we will make.

Materials   Workpiece from the last demonstration.

Tools   Top and bottom fullers of equal radius.

ACTIONS

1. Show fullers to trainees.

2. Mark a point 100mm from the end of the rod with a piece of chalk.

3. Place the rod in the hearth so that the chalk mark is in the centre of the
    fire, and heat it up to a yellow heat.

4. Check tools are in the correct position.

5. Bring the rod out and place the chalk mark over the bottom fuller.

6. Place the top fuller over the bottom fuller, and strike it with a sledge-
    hammer. Make sure that the rod is at right angles to the fullers.

7. Twist the rod through 90 degrees and repeat until a distinct neck has been
    formed.

POINTS FOR EMPHASIS

o Do not let the metal become too hot and melt.
o Top and bottom fullers must be placed directly over each other.
o The rod must be positioned at 90 degrees to the fullers.

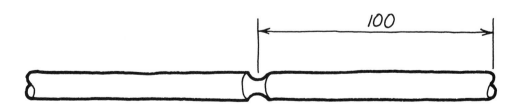

DEMO 5 Forming a tight curve

Why   This technique will be used to form the bends on the carpenters' brace.

Materials Workpiece from the last demonstration.

Tools   Centre punch; ruler; hand-hammer; small water container.

ACTIONS

1. Use a centre punch to mark a point 50mm from the end of the rod.

2. Place the rod in the hearth so that the punch mark is in the centre of the fire, and heat it up to a yellow heat.

3. Remove the rod and quench the heat 12mm either side of the punch mark, using the quenching tank and the water container.

4. Place one end of the rod into the hole in the anvil, and bend it through 90 degrees.

POINTS FOR EMPHASIS

o Do not let the metal become too hot and melt.
o Steel bends wherever it is hottest.

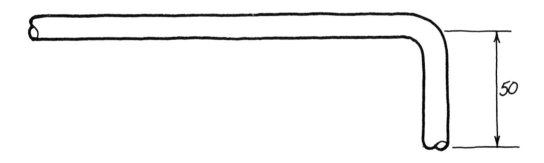

DEMO 6   Upsetting

Why   This technique is used when making a carpenters' brace.

Materials   Workpiece from the last demonstration.

Tools   Forging hammer.

ACTIONS

1.   Heat the end of the rod up to a bright yellow heat.

2.   Quench the rod using the water container, leaving only the first 50mm at forging heat.

3.   Hold the rod upright on the anvil and strike the end sharply with the hand hammer.

4.   Correct any bending as soon as it appears.

5.   Repeat this process until the end of the rod is 20mm in diameter.

POINTS FOR EMPHASIS

o   The steel will deform wherever it is hottest.
o   Correct any bending as soon as it forms, and forge out any creases as these may form cracks later.

DEMO 7   The use of a hot set

Why   This technique will be used when making a plane blade.

Materials   One piece of mild steel 200 × 25 × 12mm (or any piece of
                 plate over 4mm thick).

Tools   Sledgehammer; hot set.

ACTIONS

1. Show hot set to trainees.

2. Choose a volunteer to use the sledgehammer.

3. Heat the bar up to a yellow heat and place it on the cutting block of the
    anvil.

4. Using a hot set and a sledgehammer cut the bar into two equal parts.
    Position the hot set at an angle, and when it is in the right place bring it up
    into a vertical position so it can be struck with the sledgehammer.

5. Quench hot set in water every third stroke.

6. Cut almost right through on the cutting block of the anvil. Position the cut
    along the edge of the anvil; use the hot set and anvil as the two blades in a
    pair of shears.

POINTS FOR EMPHASIS

○ Hot sets are thinner than cold sets and have a finer cutting edge.
○ Quench the hot set to keep it cool and maintain its edge.
○ Do not let metal become so hot that it melts.
○ Do not cut on the face of the anvil as it may become marked.
○ Only when the hot set is vertical should the striker hit it with the sledge
   hammer.

Workshop lesson: Tongs

Tongs are needed to hold small pieces of metal that are too hot to hold in the hand.

1. Tongs are usually made by the blacksmith and consist of two pieces of forged steel pivoted on a rivet, like a pair of pliers.

2. The portion of metal around the rivet is called the eye.

3. The handles, or reins, are at least 300mm long to prevent the smith's hand getting too close to the fire.

4. They are made to many different designs depending on the work they are required to do.

5. Round mouth tongs are made to fit rods, flat tongs are made to fit flat bars. Whenever a new job is started, check that the tongs hold the workpiece tightly.

6. Always hold the mouth so that it opens vertically, never from side to side. This prevents the workpiece from spinning out and injuring somebody when it is struck with a hammer.

7. Always keep the tongs cool. Never let them get red hot unless they need to be adjusted.

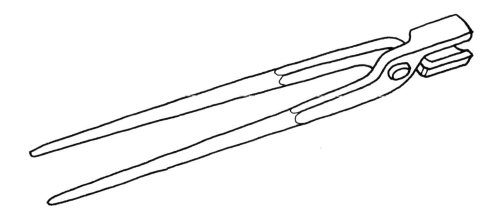

DEMO 8   To adjust a pair of tongs

Why   So that the workpiece is held safely in the jaws.

Materials   Scrap timber 40mm wide; workpiece.

Tools   Forging hammer; one pair of tongs.

ACTIONS

1. Heat the eye up to a yellow heat.

2. Remove the tongs and place a piece of timber between the reins. (Cool the reins if necessary.)

3. Place the workpiece in the mouth and close the jaws around the workpiece with light hammer blows.

POINTS FOR EMPHASIS

o   Do not let the tongs become too hot and melt.
o   The piece of timber prevents the distance between the two reins from becoming too small.

Workshop lesson: Hardening

Why   In order to make an effective cutting tool the correct type of steel must be hardened.

Materials   One piece of $150 \times 20 \times 4mm$ high carbon steel.

Tools   Forging hammer; quenching tank; flat mouth tongs; fine file.

ACTIONS

1. Heat the steel up to a cherry red.

2. Quench it in water.

3. Hold the steel in a pair of tongs over the edge of the anvil and hit it with a hammer.

4. File it with a fine file.

POINTS FOR EMPHASIS

o   Carbon steel has a higher percentage of carbon than mild steel. This makes it ideal for use in cutting edge tools.
o   The steel has become so hard it breaks like glass with the slightest tap, and cannot be filed.
o   This is the first stage in the heat treatment of carbon steel tools.

QUESTIONS

■   Can a piece of steel treated in this way make a good cutting tool?
■   How can a chisel forged from high carbon steel and hardened be made tougher to withstand hammer blows?

Workshop lesson: Tempering

Why   Tempering is the second process in heat-treating carbon steel. It makes the steel slightly less hard, but much stronger, and imbues the steel with a number of different properties.

Materials   One piece of high carbon steel 150 × 20 × 4mm.

Tools   Tongs; container for shallow water-quenching; a piece of heavy section steel.

ACTIONS

1. Heat the heavy section of steel up to a yellow heat.

2. Harden the small piece of carbon steel.

3. Clean off the oxide with a brick or a broken grinding stone, until the metal is shiny.

4. Take the heavy section of steel out of the fire and place the carbon steel on top of it so that a few centimetres hang over the edge.

5. Wait for the tempering colours to appear.

6. When all the colours are showing (from straw to blue), quench the steel in water.

QUESTIONS

- Which colour denotes the hottest temperature?
- Where is the hardest part of the sample piece?

NOTE: Pale straw is the colour used for most carpentry tools.

Introduction to blacksmithing   179

Workshop lesson: Annealing

Why Annealing will allow high carbon steel to be filed, cut or bent cold. This must be done directly after the tool has been forged, and before it is filed.

Materials Small piece of carbon steel; box of ashes.

Tools Tongs.

ACTIONS

1. Heat the steel slowly up to a red heat.

2. Bury it immediately in the box of ashes or in the coals beside the fire.

POINTS FOR EMPHASIS

○ This process allows the steel to cool down very slowly and leaves it in its softest state.

○ Small items should be annealed or buried alongside a large piece of heated steel or they will cool too quickly, even in ashes.

Workshop lesson: Cutting edge tools

The cutting edge tools described in these demonstration plans include:

o   10mm mortise chisel
o   25mm chisel
o   One-piece plane blade
o   20mm centre bit

In addition there are instructions for making a simple carpenters' brace, but this is not an edge tool.

   Once the techniques for making these tools have been learnt they can be used to produce cutting tools of any size or design, but a number of basic rules must be applied to all similar tools.

o   The back of all cutting edge tools must be smooth if it is to sharpen to a good edge.

WHY?   If the back of the tool has pits in the surface the cutting edge will be jagged.

o   Mortising chisels must have parallel sides.

WHY?   If the blade gets thicker towards the handle it will bind in the mortise and may split the workpiece.

o   Plane blades must be straight.

WHY?   If a plane blade is twisted or bent it will not lie flat on the frog of the plane and will chatter or vibrate in use.

o   Cutting edge tools must be forged from high carbon steel.

WHY?   Ordinary mild steel cannot be hardened and tempered sufficiently.

High carbon steel can be obtained in the form of scrap from the parts of motor vehicles and agricultural machines. Choose those parts that have been made to withstand wear or shock, such as springs, drive shafts and plough discs.

o   Cutting edge tools must be hardened and tempered if they are to work well.

WHY?   A blade that is too soft will blunt quickly; one that is too hard will chip.

PLANE BLADE

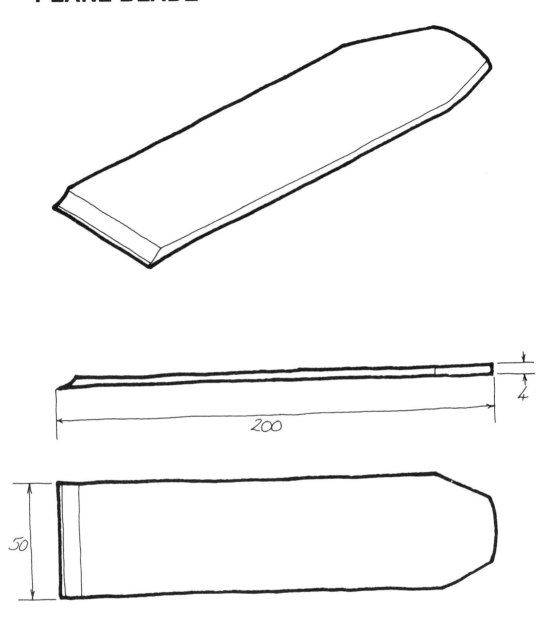

Objective

At the end of this session each participant will have made a plane blade.

Previous knowledge assumed

Basic skills, including use of a hot set and drawing down.

Tools and materials

Leaf spring 4mm thick
Hot set
Combination flat/round tongs
Hand-hammer
Sledgehammer
Old file
Flatter
Piece of old grinding wheel
Container for shallow water quenching
Ruler or tape measure

Common problems

Failure to quench set
Burning metal
Incorrect working temperature
Quenching at wrong temperature when hardening

Introduction

Time   One day.

What   In this session we are all going to make a plane blade.

Why   The blade we are going to make is a simple one-piece cutter that can be used in the wooden plane also described in these demonstration plans. Cutting the slot for a cap iron is quite a difficult operation, but after you have practised a little more you may like to try on your own.

How   The session will be made up of a series of demonstrations. Each step will be demonstrated two or three times. I will ask some questions to check that the demonstration was clear, then you will practise the same operation. We will wait until everyone is finished before the next step is demonstrated.

This is the blade we are going to make. [SHOW TOOL TO TRAINEES] It fits into the plane like this.

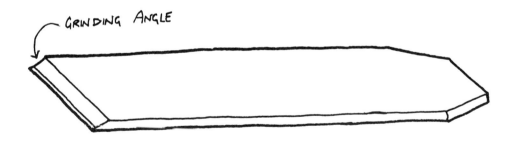

DEMO 1   Cutting out the blank

Why   So that the blade can be forged to shape.

Materials   One piece of 4mm thick leaf spring.

Tools   Sledgehammer; hot set; flat tongs; chalk; ruler.

ACTIONS

1. Mark a point on the anvil 180mm from one end with a piece of chalk.

2. Work the steel at an orange heat.

3. Mark the length of the blade with the hot set from the chalk mark on the anvil.

4. Mark a point on the spring, 50mm from one side using a ruler, a hot set and sledgehammer.

5. Cut the blade to length and width, holding the hot set over the edge of the anvil when finishing the cut.

POINTS FOR EMPHASIS

o Do not burn the metal; otherwise it will not harden and temper properly.
o Use the cutting face of the anvil.
o Use the edge of the anvil and the hot set like a pair of shears.

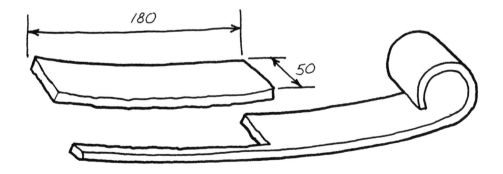

Squaring up the blade

Why   To reduce the amount of filing needed to finish the blade.

Materials Workpiece from the last demonstration.

Tools   Flat tongs; old file; hot set; sledgehammer; forging hammer.

ACTIONS

1. Work the steel at an orange heat.

2. Cut off the top corners with a sledgehammer and hot set.

3. File off the jagged edges with an old file.

4. Hold the blade at a slight angle on the anvil and forge the edges square with a hand hammer. Check that the sides are parallel.

5. Hold the end of the blade up to forge in the corners at the top.

POINTS FOR EMPHASIS

○ If the jagged edges are forged into the blade they may form cracks later.
○ It is important that the two sides are parallel so that the blade fits into the plane easily.

DEMO 3   Forging the grinding angle

Why   To reduce the amount of filing needed to finish the blade.

Materials   Workpiece from the last demonstration.

Tools   Flat tongs; flatter (if available); forging hammer; sledge-hammer.

ACTIONS

1. Work the steel at an orange heat.

2. Hold the end of the blade near the edge of the anvil and forge in the grinding angle of the blade.

3. Use a flatter and sledgehammer to true up the sides and edges of the blade.

4. Anneal the blade by heating it up to a red heat and burying it in the ashes close to the fire to cool down slowly.

POINTS FOR EMPHASIS

o   When forging the grinding angle the blade should be held near the edge of the anvil so that the hammer can be brought down at an angle without hitting the face of the anvil.
o   It is very important to forge the blade as flat and straight as possible.
o   Annealing the steel makes it soft enough to file, ready for the next stage.

DEMO 4   Filing the blade

Why   So that the blade can be sharpened effectively.

Materials   Workpiece from the last demonstration.

Tools   Large half-round file; metalwork vice; ruler/straight edge.

ACTIONS

1.   Clamp the blade in the vice with the back of the blade on top.

2.   File across the blade to make it flat and draw file it to make it smooth.

3.   File the second side in the same way.

4.   File the edges straight and parallel.

5.   File the grinding angle.

POINTS FOR EMPHASIS

○   When draw filing the file should be held with forefingers and thumbs over the centre of the blade to prevent the file rocking, and keep the blade as flat as possible.

○   The first 50mm of the side that forms the cutting edge must be filed until there are no depressions; otherwise the blade cannot be sharpened properly.

DEMO 5 — Hardening and tempering

Why To give the cutting edge the correct hardness and durability.

Materials Plane blade; heavy section steel.

Tools Flat mouth tongs; fine file; abrasive stone; quenching tank; container for shallow water quenching.

ACTIONS

1. Heat the heavy section steel up to a yellow heat.

2. Heat the first 30mm of the cutting edge to a dull red heat.

3. Quench the blade, holding it vertically in the water.

4. Test the hardness with a fine file and polish off the oxide with the abrasive stone.

5. Remove the heavy section steel from the fire and position the blade on top so that the cutting edge overhangs by about 20mm.

6. When the tip of the blade turns pale yellow, quench the tip in a shallow dish of water and let the rest of the blade cool down slowly.

7. The blade can now be ground and sharpened.

POINTS FOR EMPHASIS

o If the blade is quenched at an angle during the hardening process it may warp.

o When the blade has been properly hardened the file should just slide off.

o The oxide must be removed so that the tempering colours can be seen.

25MM CHISEL

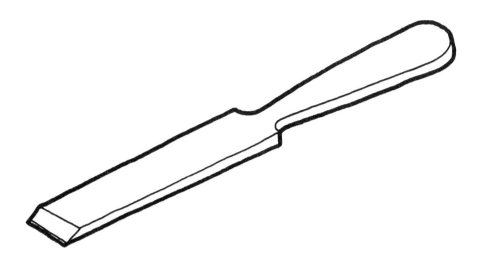

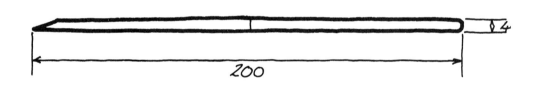

200

4

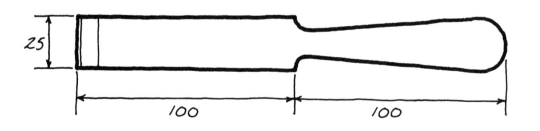

25

100

100

190   *25mm chisel*

Objective

At the end of this session each participant will have made a 25mm chisel.

Previous knowledge assumed

Basic skills, including use of a hot set, top and bottom fullers and drawing down.

Tools and materials

Leaf spring 4mm thick
Hot set
Combination flat/round tongs
Hand-hammer
Sledgehammer
Top and bottom fullers
Piece of old grinding wheel
Container for shallow water quenching
Ruler or tape measure

Common problems

Failure to quench set
Burning the metal
Incorrect working temperature
Quenching at wrong temperature when hardening

Introduction

Time   One day.

What   In this session we are all going to make a 25mm chisel.

Why   Although not an essential tool, a 25mm chisel is good for general purpose work such as trimming tenons or paring back sockets. This type of chisel can also be used as the blade for the wooden rebate plane described in these session plans.

How   The session will be made up of a series of demonstrations. Each step will be demonstrated two or three times. I will ask some questions to check that the demonstration was clear, then you will practise the same operation. We will wait until everyone is finished before the next step is demonstrated.

This is the chisel we are going to make [SHOW TOOL TO TRAINEES]. You use it in the same way as a manufactured chisel except that you use a hammer for striking the handle. Inner tube rubber can be wrapped around the handle to make it more comfortable to hold.

These are the parts.

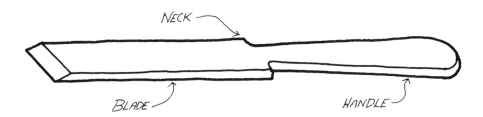

DEMO 1   Cutting out the blank

Why   So that the chisel can be forged to shape.

Materials   One piece of 4mm thick leaf spring.

Tools   Sledgehammer; hot set; flat tongs; chalk; ruler.

ACTIONS

1. Mark a point on the anvil 180mm from one end with a piece of chalk.

2. Work the steel at an orange heat.

3. Mark the length of the chisel with a hot set from the chalk mark on the anvil.

4. Mark a point on the spring 25mm from one side using a ruler, a hot set and sledgehammer.

5. Cut the blade to length and width, holding the hot set over the edge of the anvil when finishing the cut.

POINTS FOR EMPHASIS

o The metal will not harden and temper properly if it is allowed to burn.
o Use the cutting face of the anvil.
o Use the edge of the anvil and the hot set like a pair of shears.

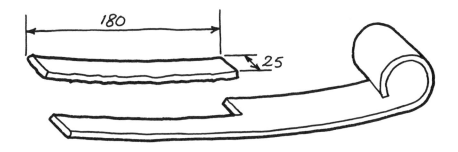

25mm chisel   193

DEMO 2   Squaring up the blade

Why   To reduce the amount of filing needed to finish the blade.

Materials   Workpiece from the last demonstration.

Tools   Flat tongs; old file; forging hammer.

ACTIONS

1. Work the steel at an orange heat.

2. File off the jagged edges with an old file.

3. Hold the blade at a slight angle on the anvil and forge the edges square with a hand-hammer. Check that the sides are parallel.

POINTS FOR EMPHASIS

o If the jagged edges are forged into the blade they may form cracks later.
o It is important that the two sides are parallel, particularly if the blade is to be used for a rebate plane.

DEMO 3 Forging the neck

Why   This makes it easier to forge the handle and to file the blade.

Materials   Workpiece from the last demonstration.

Tools   Square mouth tongs; top and bottom fullers; sledgehammer; ruler; chalk.

ACTIONS

1. Mark a chalk line on the anvil 90mm from one edge.

2. Place the bottom fuller in the anvil.

3. Work the steel at an orange heat.

4. Use the chalk mark to gauge the length of the handle and position the chisel on the fuller. Position the top fuller directly over the bottom fuller and strike with a sledgehammer.

5. Turn the chisel through 180 degrees and strike again.

6. Repeat until the neck is about 12mm thick.

POINTS FOR EMPHASIS

o Top and bottom fullers must be placed directly over each other.
o The chisel must be positioned at 90 degrees to the fullers.

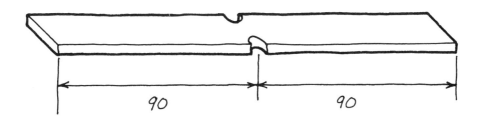

DEMO 4 Forging the handle

Why   So that it is comfortable to hold.

Materials   Workpiece from the last demonstration.

Tools   Square mouth tongs; forging hammer.

ACTIONS

1. Work the steel at an orange heat.

2. Hold the neck of the chisel over the edge of the anvil with the blade pointing slightly downwards.

3. Draw down the handle to blend in with the neck, twisting the chisel through 180 degrees every few blows, to form an even taper. Bring the hammer down at a slight angle.

4. Forge a radius at the end of the handle.

5. Chamfer the corners with light blows.

POINTS FOR EMPHASIS

o Keep the blade of the chisel away from the edge of the anvil so that the sides are not marked.

o The face of the anvil forms one side of the taper, while the hammer forms the other side.

DEMO 5 **Forging the blade**

Why   So that it will cut accurately.

Materials   Workpiece from the last demonstration.

Tools   Square mouth tongs; forging hammer; sledgehammer; flatter (if available).

ACTIONS

1. Work the steel at an orange heat.

2. Forge a slight taper in the blade so that it becomes thicker towards the handle.

3. Forge the sides of the blade parallel and to a width of 25mm.

4. Hold the end of the chisel over the edge of the anvil, and forge the grinding angle.

5. Use a sledgehammer and a flatter to make the sides and edges of the chisel straight and flat.

6. Anneal the blade by heating it up to a red heat and burying it in the ashes close to the fire to cool down slowly.

POINTS FOR EMPHASIS

○ When forging the grinding angle the blade should be held near the edge of the anvil so that the hammer can be brought down at an angle without hitting the face of the anvil.
○ It is very important to forge the blade as flat and straight as possible.
○ Annealing the steel makes it soft enough to file ready for the next stage.

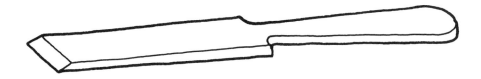

25mm chisel   197

DEMO 6   Filing the blade

Why   So that the blade can be sharpened effectively.

Materials   Workpiece from the last demonstration.

Tools   Large half-round file; metalwork vice; ruler/straight edge.

ACTIONS

1. Clamp the blade in the vice with the back of the blade on top.

2. File across the blade to make it flat and draw file it to make it smooth.

3. File the second side in the same way.

4. File the edges straight and parallel.

5. File the grinding angle.

POINTS FOR EMPHASIS

o   When draw filing the file should be held with forefingers and thumbs over the centre of the blade to prevent the file rocking, and to keep the blade as flat as possible.

o   The first 50mm of the side that forms the cutting edge must be filed until there are no depressions.

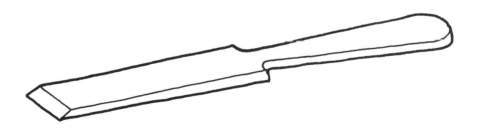

198   *25mm chisel*

DEMO 7 Hardening and tempering

Why　　　　To give the cutting edge the correct hardness and durability.

Materials　　Chisel; heavy section steel.

Tools　　　Flat mouth tongs; fine file; abrasive stone; quenching tank; container for shallow water quenching.

ACTIONS

1. Heat the heavy section steel up to a yellow heat.

2. Heat the first 30mm of the cutting edge to a dull red heat.

3. Quench the blade, holding it vertically in the water.

4. Test the hardness with a fine file and polish off the oxide with the abrasive stone.

5. Remove the heavy section steel from the fire and position the blade on top so that the cutting edge overhangs by about 20mm.

6. When the tip of the blade turns pale yellow, quench the tip in a shallow dish of water and let the rest of the chisel cool down slowly.

POINTS FOR EMPHASIS

o If the blade is quenched at an angle during the hardening process it may warp.
o When the blade has been properly hardened the file should just slide off.
o The oxide must be removed so that the tempering colours can be seen.
o The blade can now be ground and sharpened.

10MM MORTISE CHISEL

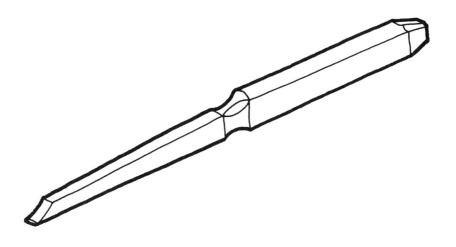

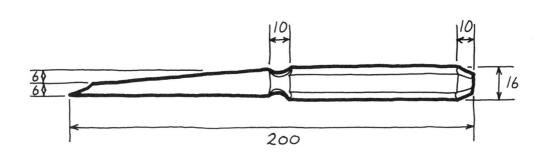

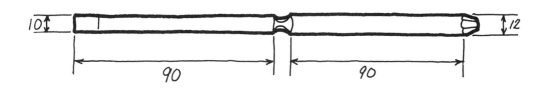

Objective

At the end of this session each participant will have made a 10mm mortise chisel.

Previous knowledge assumed

Basic skills, including use of a hot set; top and bottom fullers and drawing down.

Tools and materials

Coil spring 16mm diameter
Hot set
Combination flat/round tongs
Hand-hammer
Top and bottom fullers
Sledgehammer
Piece of old grinding wheel
Containers for shallow water quenching
Ruler or tape measure

Common problems

Failure to quench set
Burning the metal
Incorrect working temperature
Quenching at wrong temperature when hardening
Not forming parallel sides on the blade

Introduction

Time   One day.

What   In this session we are all going to make a 10mm mortise chisel.

Why   This is probably the most popular size of chisel for mortising the joints in chair and table legs. Without a mortise chisel a carpenter is unable to make some of the most sought-after items of furniture. The handle is made from the same piece of steel as the blade. This makes the tool very strong and also means that it can be struck with a hammer, making it very effective for mortising.

How   The session will be made up of a series of demonstrations. Each step will be demonstrated two or three times. I will ask some questions to check that the demonstration was clear, then you will practise the same operation. We will wait until everyone is finished before the next step is demonstrated.

This is the mortise chisel we are going to make [SHOW TOOL TO TRAINEES]. You use it in the same way as a manufactured chisel except that you strike the handle with a hammer.

These are the parts.

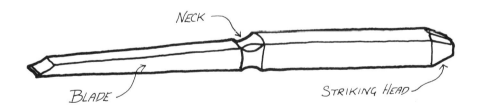

DEMO 1   Cutting off the blank

Why   So that the chisel can be forged to shape.

Materials   One piece of 16mm diameter coil spring.

Tools   Sledgehammer; hot set; round tongs; chalk; ruler.

ACTIONS

1. Mark a point on the anvil 180mm from one end with a piece of chalk.

2. Work the steel at an orange heat.

3. Roll the spring up to the mark on the anvil and cut the blank off with a hot set and sledgehammer. Cut most of the way through, then bend the steel until it breaks.

4. Straighten the blank by placing it in the hardie hole and bending it. Small adjustments should be made with the hand-hammer.

POINTS FOR EMPHASIS

o The metal will not harden and temper properly if it is allowed to burn.
o Use the cutting face of the anvil.

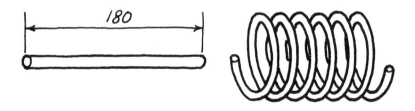

DEMO 2   Forging the striking head and the handle

Why   The point at the end of the handle allows the chisel to be
               struck squarely and prevents it from mushrooming. The
               shape of the handle prevents it from twisting in your hand
               during use.

Materials   Workpiece from the last demonstration.

Tools   Forging hammer; round-mouth tongs.

ACTIONS

1. Work the steel at an orange heat.

2. Hold the reins of the tongs against the side of your legs and square up the
    end of the workpiece by striking it with a hand-hammer.

3. Flatten the side of the handle for half the length of the blank. The handle
    should be about 12mm thick and 16mm wide when finished.

4. Draw down the striking head to a 10mm long point with a flat area on the
    end.

POINTS FOR EMPHASIS

○ Make sure the ends of the tongs do not stick into your legs.
○ Do not make the handle too thin.
○ Drawing down the striking end of the chisel helps to direct the shock of the
   hammer blow down the centre of the tool.

DEMO 3 Forging the neck

Why   This makes it easier to forge and file the handle.

Materials   Workpiece from the last demonstration.

Tools   Round-mouth tongs; top and bottom fullers; sledgehammer;
               ruler; chalk.

ACTIONS

1. Mark a chalk line on the anvil 90mm from one edge.

2. Place the bottom fuller in the anvil.

3. Work the steel at an orange heat.

4. Use the chalk mark to gauge the length of the handle and position the
    chisel on the fuller. Position the top fuller directly over the bottom fuller
    and strike with a sledgehammer.

5. Turn the chisel through 90 degrees and strike again.

6. Repeat until the neck is about 12mm thick.

POINTS FOR EMPHASIS

o Top and bottom fullers must be placed directly over each other.
o The chisel must be positioned at 90 degrees to the fullers.

10mm mortise chisel 205

DEMO 4   Forging the blade

Why   So that the chisel will cut an accurate mortise.

Materials   Workpiece from the last demonstration.

Tools   Forging hammer; round-mouth tongs; hot set.

ACTIONS

1. Work the steel at an orange heat.

2. Forge the blade into a square section.

3. Forge the blade to 10mm width making sure the sides are parallel. The thickness of the chisel should taper slightly from the handle to the cutting edge.

4. Cut the blade to about 100mm in length and forge in the grinding angle.

5. Straighten out the blade and the handle, using a hand hammer only.

6. Anneal the blade by heating it up to a red heat and burying it in the ashes close to the fire to cool down slowly.

POINTS FOR EMPHASIS

o   The sides of the blade must be parallel; otherwise it will bind in the mortise.

o   Annealing the steel makes it soft enough to file ready for the next stage.

DEMO 5 Filing the blade

Why So that the blade can be sharpened effectively.

Materials Workpiece from the last demonstration.

Tools Large half-round file; metalwork vice; ruler/straight edge.

ACTIONS

1. Clamp the blade in the vice with the back of the blade on top.

2. File across the blade to make it flat and draw file it to make it smooth.

3. File the second side in the same way.

4. File the edges straight and parallel.

5. File the grinding angle.

POINTS FOR EMPHASIS

○ When draw filing the file should be held with forefingers and thumbs over the centre of the blade to prevent the file rocking, and to keep the blade as flat as possible.
○ The first 50mm of the side that forms the cutting edge must be filed until there are no depressions.

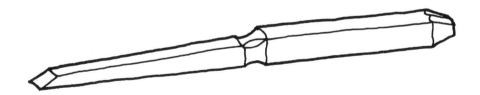

DEMO 6   Hardening and tempering

Why   To give the cutting edge the correct hardness and durability.

Materials   Chisel; heavy section steel.

Tools   Round-mouth tongs; fine file; abrasive stone; quenching tank; container for shallow water quenching.

ACTIONS

1. Heat the heavy section steel up to a yellow heat.

2. Heat the first 30mm of the cutting edge to a dull red heat.

3. Quench the blade, holding it vertically in the water.

4. Test the hardness with a fine file, and polish off the oxide with the abrasive stone.

5. Remove the heavy section steel from the fire and position the blade on top so that the cutting edge overhangs by about 20mm.

6. When the tip of the blade turns pale yellow, quench the tip in a shallow dish of water and let the rest of the chisel cool down slowly.

POINTS FOR EMPHASIS

o If the blade is quenched at an angle during the hardening process it may warp.
o When the blade has been properly hardened the file should just slide off.
o The oxide must be removed so that the tempering colours can be seen.
o The blade can now be ground and sharpened.

CARPENTERS' BRACE

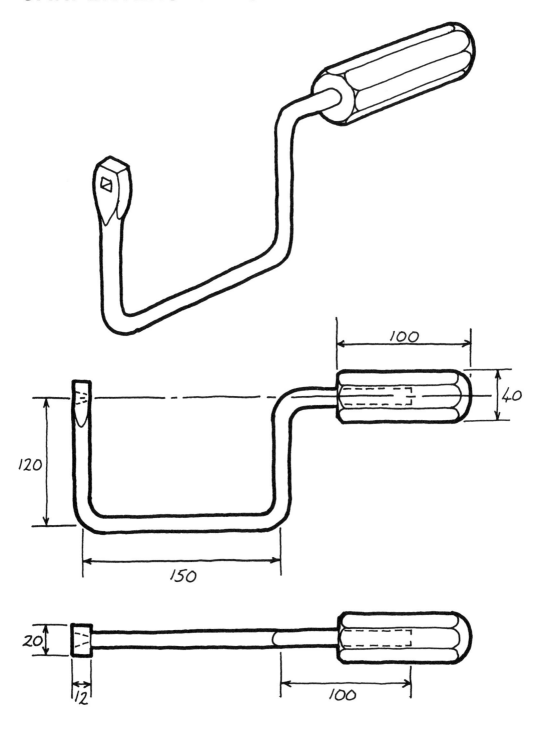

Objective

At the end of this session each participant will have made a carpenters' brace.

Previous knowledge assumed

Basic skills, including use of a hot set; bending and drawing down.

Tools and materials

One piece of 12mm mild steel rod 600mm long
One piece of 12mm spring steel rod 150mm long
Large hexagonal nut
Combination flat/round tongs
Hand-hammer
Sledgehammer
Hot set
Water container
Ruler or tape measure

Common problems

Failure to quench set
Burning the metal
Incorrect working temperature
Upsetting the end
Punching the hole off centre
Bending the crank the wrong way

Introduction

Time   One day.

What   In this session we are all going to make a simple carpenters' brace.

Why   Carpenters' braces are usually expensive to buy and the chucks, which are quite delicate, can break easily. The chuck on this brace is forged from one piece of metal and will not break.

How   The session will be made up of a series of demonstrations. Each step will be demonstrated two or three times. I will ask some questions to check that the demonstration was clear, then you will practise the same operation. We will wait until everyone is finished before the next step is demonstrated.

This is the brace we are going to make [SHOW TOOL TO TRAINEES]. These are the parts.

It works like this.

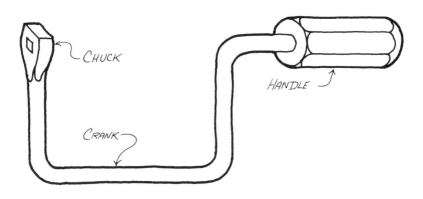

DEMO 1   Upsetting the chuck

Why   So that the chuck will be strong enough to resist the turning forces.

Materials   One piece of 12mm diameter mild steel rod 600 mm long.

Tools   Forging hammer; small water container.

ACTIONS

1. Work the steel at a bright yellow heat.

2. Quench the rod using the water container, leaving only the first 50mm at forging heat.

3. Hold the rod upright on the anvil and strike the end sharply with the hand-hammer.

4. Correct any bending as soon as it appears.

5. Repeat this process until the end of the rod is 20mm in diameter.

POINTS FOR EMPHASIS

o   The steel will deform wherever it is hottest.
o   Correct any bending as soon as it forms, and forge out any creases as these may form cracks later.

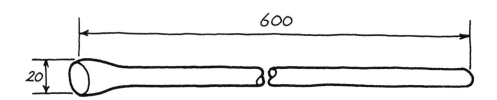

DEMO 2   Forging the chuck

Why   So that the chuck hole can be punched.

Materials   Workpiece from the last demonstration.

Tools   Forging hammer.

ACTIONS

1. Work the steel at a bright yellow heat.

2. Flatten the upset end to a thickness of not less than 12mm.

3. Square up the sides over the bick of the anvil.

4. Square up the end by holding the rod against your leg and striking the end.

5. Check that the chuck is in line with the rod.

POINTS FOR EMPHASIS

o   The thickness of the chuck should not be less than 12mm to give adequate grip to the bit.

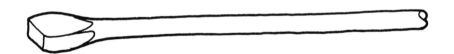

DEMO 3   Forging the square punch

Why　　　　　So that the hole in the chuck can be punched.

Materials　　One piece of 12mm diameter coil spring, 150mm long.

Tools　　　　Hot set; sledgehammer; forging hammer.

ACTIONS

1.   Work the steel at an orange heat.

2.   Cut off 150mm of coil spring and straighten it out.

3.   Place the steel close to the edge of the anvil. Forge the striking end of the punch by drawing down a 10mm-long point with a flat on the end.

4.   Forge the punch end into a square point with a taper equal to the square shank on an auger bit. Start at the end and work back until it is the correct shape.

POINTS FOR EMPHASIS

o   Drawing down the striking end of the punch helps to direct the shock of the hammer blow down the centre of the tool.

o   Giving the punch the same taper as the shank of an auger bit will allow you to use most manufactured augers in the brace.

DEMO 4   Punching the chuck

Why So that the drill bit can be fitted to the brace.

Materials Workpiece from demonstration 2.

Tools Forging hammer; large hexagonal nut; square tapered punch.

ACTIONS

1. Heat the chuck to a yellow heat.

2. Place the chuck on the anvil and position the punch in the centre of one flat face.

3. Drive the punch into the chuck until a dark spot appears on the other side. Make sure the punch is upright. Quench the punch after every third blow.

4. Turn the chuck over. Position the punch in the centre of the dark spot and drive the punch until a small piece of steel is removed.

5. Place the nut over the hole in the anvil; from one side only, open out the hole in the chuck until it is about 10mm square.

6. Drive the punch into the hole four times, each time twisting the punch through 90 degrees.

7. Tidy and straighten up the chuck.

POINTS FOR EMPHASIS

o Open out the hole from one side only to give an evenly tapered chuck.
o Twisting the punch four times through 90 degrees makes all sides of the chuck even.

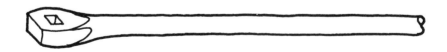

DEMO 5   Bending the handle

Why   This will form the 'crank' in the brace, which will allow the
               bit to be turned.

Materials   Workpiece from the last demonstration.

Tools   Centre punch; ruler; forging hammer; small water container.

ACTIONS

1. Use a centre punch to mark a point on the side of the rod 120mm from the
    centre of the chuck.

2. Heat the rod to a bright yellow heat. Quench the rod 12mm either side of
    the centre punch mark. Place the rod in the hole in the anvil, making sure
    that the side of the chuck with the small hole is on the inside of the crank,
    and bend the rod through 90 degrees.

3. Mark a point 150mm from the first bend with a centre punch, and bend the
    rod as before.

4. Lay the brace flat on the anvil, with the centre of the chuck in line with the
    edge and the crank parallel to the same edge. Mark the position of the
    final bend.

5. Bend as before, but make sure the top of the brace lines up with the hole
    in the chuck. Final adjustments can be made with a hand-hammer.

POINTS FOR EMPHASIS

○   Marking the side of the rod will prevent cracking as the rod is bent.
○   All the bends should be at right angles and in the same plane.
○   The top of the brace must line up with the hole in the chuck; otherwise the
    drill will turn eccentrically.

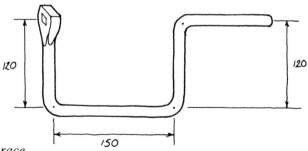

216   *Carpenters' brace*

Making the handle

[The handle is made from timber so the class will have to return to the woodwork shop to use the carpentry tools.]

Why   So that it is comfortable to hold.

Materials   One piece of hardwood 100 × 40 × 40mm.

Tools   Ruler; pencil; marking gauge; plane; carpenters' brace; 12mm auger bit.

ACTIONS

1. Mark diagonals on one end of the handle to mark the centre of the hole.

2. Gauge lines 12mm from each edge on all four sides.

3. Plane down to the gauge lines to form an eight-sided cross-section.

4. Clamp the handle vertically in the vice and drill a 12mm hole where the diagonals meet. The hole should be at least 50mm deep.

5. Shape the top of the handle and smooth all the edges.

POINTS FOR EMPHASIS

o Ask someone to check that the drill is vertical.

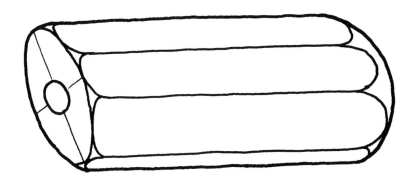

DEMO 7 Adjusting the brace

Why   So that the brace drives the bit correctly.

Materials   Scrap timber.

Tools   Completed brace; auger bit.

ACTIONS

1. Place the drill securely in the chuck and the handle on the top of the brace.

2. Begin drilling the scrap timber. Note where the brace is not in alignment.

3. Correct the alignment by clamping the brace in a vice and bending it cold.

4. Repeat until the handle is in line with the bit.

POINTS FOR EMPHASIS

o   The bit must be aligned with the handle if holes are to be drilled accurately.

20MM CENTRE BIT

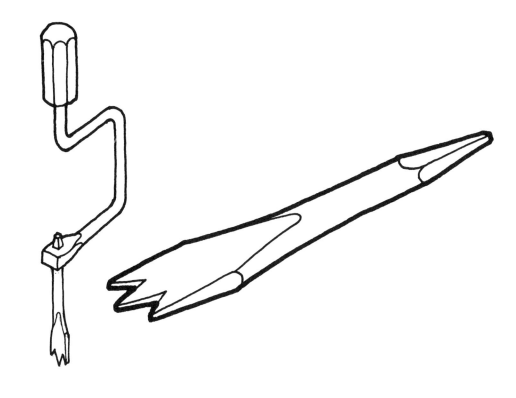

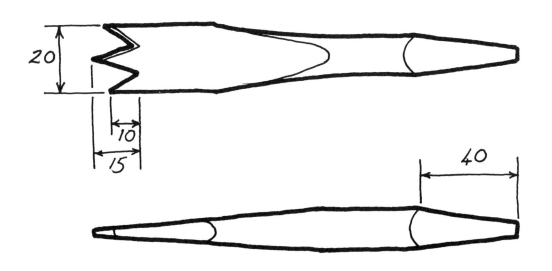

20mm centre bit 219

Objective

At the end of this session each participant will have made a 20mm centre bit.

Previous knowledge assumed

Basic skills, including use of a hot set and drawing down.

Tools and materials

Coil spring 12mm diameter
Hot set
Combination flat/round tongs
Hand-hammer
Sledgehammer
Piece of old grinding wheel
Container for shallow water quenching

Common problems

Failure to quench set
Burning the metal
Incorrect working temperature
Quenching at wrong temperature when hardening
Filing the cutting edges

Introduction

Time   One day.

What   In this session we are all going to make a 20mm centre bit for
                  the carpenters' brace.

Why   Although most industrially made auger bits will fit your
                  brace we are going to make a bit that can be made cheaply
                  and relatively easily.

How   The session will be made up of a series of demonstrations.
                  Each step will be demonstrated two or three times. I will ask
                  some questions to check that the demonstration was clear,
                  then you will practise the same operation. We will wait until
                  everyone is finished before the next step is demonstrated.

This is the bit we are going to make [SHOW TOOL TO TRAINEES]. This bit
has a scraping action rather than cutting like an auger.

It works like this.

DEMO 1   Drawing down the shank

Why   So that the bit fits into the brace.

Materials   One piece of 12mm diameter coil spring, 100mm long.

Tools   Forging hammer; round-mouth tongs.

ACTIONS

1. Work the spring at an orange heat.

2. Draw down the blank to a square point about 50mm long with a small flat on the end.

3. Forge the blank so it fits into the hole in the chuck without wobbling.

POINTS FOR EMPHASIS

o Start drawing down at the end of the workpiece and then forge the point to the correct length.

o It is important that the shank fits tightly into the chuck so that the bit does not wobble in use.

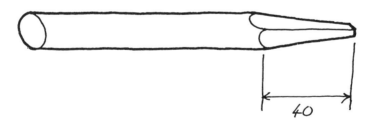

222   *20mm centre bit*

Drawing down the blade

Why   So that the cutting edge can be formed.

Materials   Workpiece from the last demonstration.

Tools   Round-mouth tongs; forging hammer.

ACTIONS

1. Work the metal at an orange heat.

2. Draw down the blade until it is just over 20mm wide, 40mm long and 3mm thick at the tip (it should taper towards the tip).

3. Forge the shank and the blade straight, using your eye to judge the alignment.

POINTS FOR EMPHASIS

o   It is very important that the blade and the shank are in line; otherwise the bit will turn eccentrically.

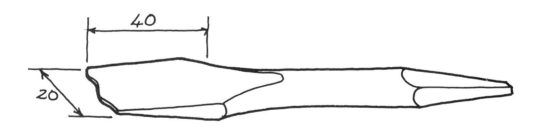

DEMO 3 Cutting the tip

Why To form the scraping edges of the bit.

Materials Workpiece from the last demonstration.

Tools Forging hammer; small, sharp hot chisel.

ACTIONS

1. Work the metal at a bright red heat.

2. Ask someone to hold the bit on the cutting block of the anvil.

3. Judge the middle, and make the two cuts on the left hand side of the bit. The centre point should be 5mm longer than the side points.

4. Turn the bit over and repeat the operation.

5. Straighten up the cutting edges of the bit.

6. Anneal the bit by heating it up to a red heat and burying it in the ashes close to the fire to cool down slowly.

POINTS FOR EMPHASIS

o The tip of the bit will cool very quickly so you may need to heat it a number of times.
o Cutting both points from the left-hand side will produce cutting edges that will need very little filing.
o Annealing the steel makes it soft enough to file ready for the next stage.

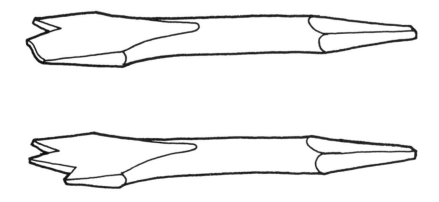

224 *20mm centre bit*

DEMO 4   Filing up the bit

Why   So that the cutting edges of the bit can be formed.

Materials   Workpiece from the last demonstration.

Tools   Metalwork vice; half-round file.

ACTIONS

1. Check that the shank fits tightly into the chuck. Correct by filing if necessary.

2. Clamp the bit in a vice; file the two faces flat and smooth, and the two sides parallel.

3. File the scraping edges at an angle of about 80 degrees. Follow the angles cut by the hot chisel.

4. File the central tip so it is in the middle of the bit.

5. Check that the central point is in the middle and that the two outside points are of the same length by fitting the bit into the brace and drilling a hole.

POINTS FOR EMPHASIS

○ If the sides are not parallel the bit may bind in the hole.
○ If the central point is not in the middle the bit will cut a larger hole.

20mm centre bit   225

DEMO 5   Hardening and tempering

Why   To give the cutting edge the correct hardness and durability.

Materials   Centre bit; heavy section steel.

Tools   Round-mouth tongs; fine file; abrasive stone; quenching
                     tank; container for shallow-water quenching.

ACTIONS

1.   Heat the heavy section steel up to a yellow heat.

2.   Heat the first 20mm of the cutting edge to a dull red heat.

3.   Quench the blade, holding it vertically in the water.

4.   Test the hardness with a fine file, and polish off the oxide with the abrasive
     stone.

5.   Remove the heavy section steel from the fire and position the blade on top
     so that the cutting edge overhangs by about 20mm.

6.   When the tip of the blade just begins to turn blue, quench the tip in a
     shallow dish of water and let the rest of the chisel cool down slowly.

POINTS FOR EMPHASIS

o   If the blade is quenched at an angle during the hardening process it may
    warp.
o   When the blade has been properly hardened the file should just slide off.
o   The oxide must be removed so that the tempering colours can be seen.
o   Tempering the bit at blue will allow you to use a file to sharpen it.